Dedication

To the memory of my father, who told me constantly that I could be anything I wanted to be; and for my daughter, Carey, who doesn't hear that message from me nearly enough.

Contents

Introduction   **4**

Design Principles   **5**

COLOR ~~~~~~~~~~~~~~~~~~~~ 6

VALUE ~~~~~~~~~~~~~~~~~~~ 10

SCALE ~~~~~~~~~~~~~~~~~~~ 12

BALANCE ~~~~~~~~~~~~~~~~ 14

UNITY ~~~~~~~~~~~~~~~~~~ 18

Design Approaches   **20**

DESIGN WALL ~~~~~~~~~~~~~~~ 20

COLLAGE CURVES ~~~~~~~~~~~~~~ 21

SLASH AND SEW ~~~~~~~~~~~~~~ 32

DESIGNING WITH A SINGLE SHAPE ~~~~~~~~~ 44

MULTI-VIEW IMAGES ~~~~~~~~~~~~ 56

IMPROVING THE CHECKERBOARD ~~~~~~~~~~~ 68

Help for Problem Quilts   **78**

WHAT'S WRONG? ~~~~~~~~~~~~~~~~ 79

Borders   **92**

NO BORDERS ~~~~~~~~~~~~~~~~~ 93

SIMPLE BORDERS ~~~~~~~~~~~~~~ 94

BINDING ~~~~~~~~~~~~~~~~~~~ 94

Ethics   **95**

Resources   **95**

Bibliography   **96**

About the Author   **96**

D0709730

Introduction

Are quilts art or craft? Should quiltmakers be considered artists? Should wall quilts demand the same prices as paintings, sculptures, and other works traditionally accepted as "fine art?"

Questions such as these swirl endlessly in the quilt arena, while more and more quilters seek to be taken seriously as artists (renaming their sewing rooms "studios"). As a teacher of quiltmaking, I am less interested in debates over definitions than I am in knowing that quilters are learning about the principles of design—and using those principles to make quilts that won't prompt these questions.

In my years of teaching quiltmaking, I have consistently asked beginning students, "What is the first thing you perceive when you walk into a room and see a quilt? What is the second, the third?" Almost always, the answers are "Color, design (or pattern), and size," in that order. Craftsmanship is at least fourth on the list.

It is not the material you have selected that matters, but the way in which you put it together—design first, last, and always.

…Take an arrangement which has only beautiful color, reduce it to black and white, and you have nothing but unrelated masses: take another which is well designed, eliminate the color, and you still have—a fine design!

John Taylor Arms and Dorothy Noyes Arms
Design in Flower Arrangement

Together, we deduce that one could make a wonderfully crafted quilt with not-so-wonderful color and design, and waste a good bit of time. I'm an advocate of great craftsmanship—in fact, I insist that my beginning students learn how to draft and use templates—but I acknowledge that craftsmanship is primarily a vehicle for color, design, and content (or "the statement"). Shouldn't quilters, then, study art with as much fervor as they develop craft?

I've observed that many people, when they were around seven or eight years old, decided they were not artists—usually because the kid sitting next to them in the third grade could draw a horse and they could not. And that was that. Thereafter, they assigned themselves the label "Non-Artist." I've always attempted to prove to quiltmaking students that, indeed, they could be artists—or at the very least, greatly improve their design skills. Design can be taught, just as chemistry and psychology can be taught.

Most quilters know what content they wish to express. (For some of us who came of age as artists in the 1960s, when abstract expressionism was the style, form *was* content.) Content abounds. What today's quilters need now, after studying technique and craftsmanship for two decades, is to learn design principles—the visual elements that give structure to expression.

People want to find organization in the things they see. If they can't, they lose interest and walk away. As quilt artists, we need to understand how to create visual unity, a visually integrated system—a visual "cosmos," so to speak.

In this book, I present simple principles that will help you create wonderful quilts, whatever your style or technique. Along with the design principles, I offer five technical "contexts," that is, five styles in which to practice and refine design principles. Some methods are my own inventions, others are new looks at techniques that have been around for a long time. Add them to your bag of tricks so you can pull out both the techniques and design principles that best shape your expressions.

Design Principles

Classes and books for quilters abound. Most of them teach technique: how to match points better, cut fabric faster, appliqué fancy shapes in dozens of different ways. But technique is simply a vehicle for getting where we're going. Imagine a concert pianist performing for her audience by playing scales. Her technique is superb. Her fingers hit every note correctly, at record speed, in perfect time. Her audience is impressed by her technical skill, but left with an empty feeling. "So what?"

Haven't we been to quilt shows with aisle upon aisle of skillfully crafted quilts that left us unmoved? Maybe the colors were predictable and boring, the compositions uncompelling. Perhaps some quilts looked as though the maker spent her energy on the main part only to resignedly add a 10"-wide single-fabric border just to qualify it for the big-quilt category.

Technique alone is not enough. Yes, we need all the techniques we can learn. We need to collect dozens of different ways to appliqué and piece fancy shapes so we can best build the design we've chosen. But it's the visual structure of the piece—arrangement, composition, design—that gives us a sense of harmony. If we learn a few of the most important elements of good design and apply them, we can go a long way toward improving our quilts, whether we make them in a traditional style or start from scratch to design innovative ones.

An artist who creates rather than imitates expresses himself; *his works are not reflections of nature but, instead, new realities, which are no less significant than the realities of nature itself.*

Kasimir Malevich
The Non Objective World

Color

Color moves us. Color shocks us. Color excites or annoys us. Sometimes color even leaves us cold. There is so much emotion tied up in color, it's often difficult to address objectively. In her book *Color: The Quilter's Guide* (That Patchwork Place, 1997), Christine Barnes gives well-researched information and inspiration to guide our study of this huge and important subject. Go outside the quilting arena, too, in your search for color education. Johannes Itten, the great German color theorist, is an indispensable source. (See the Bibliography on page 96 for other books about color.)

Because others have done such wonderful work in writing about color, I'll limit my comments to a few tidy facts and a couple of personal and sweeping opinions.

There are several approaches to organizing color—some related to color in light, others to color in pigment. The one most of us are familiar with is the twelve-section color wheel in which red, yellow, and blue are the primary colors; violet, orange, and green the secondary colors; and red-orange, yellow-orange, yellow-green, blue-green, blue-violet, and red-violet the tertiary colors.

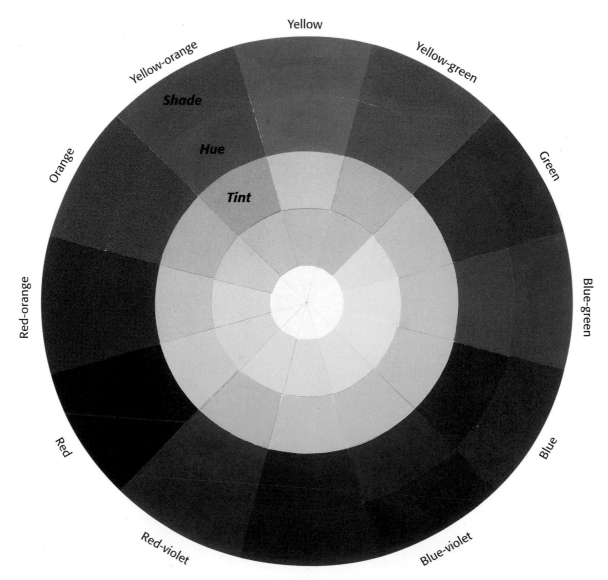

Colors, or hues, can be modified in value (relative lightness or darkness) by the addition of white or black. Adding white to a color produces a tint of the color; adding black produces a shade. Naturally, it's possible to make an infinite number of tints or shades by modulating the amount of white or black added to a color.

Intense colors

■ *Intensity* refers to brightness, or degree of purity. To decrease the intensity of a pure color, add black, white (or gray), or add the color lying directly opposite on the color wheel (the color's complement).

   Certain color schemes and palettes help us achieve different looks.

Grayed colors

■ *Achromatic* means "without color." If you made an achromatic quilt, it would be black, white, and/or any value of gray. Black and white don't count as colors.

■ *Monochromatic* means "one color." Tints and shades of a color do count as that color, so you could make a quilt of pale blue, light blue, royal blue, dark blue, and navy blue—and add black, white, or gray—and still have a monochromatic quilt.

■ *Analogous* colors lie next to each other on the color wheel. Red, red-orange, orange, yellow-orange, and yellow (plus any shades or tints of these colors) would qualify as an analogous color scheme.

Monochromatic color scheme

Achromatic color scheme

Analogous color scheme

Two complementary color schemes

Two triadic color schemes

Two triadic color schemes

Polychromatic color scheme

■ *Complementary colors* lie opposite each other on the color wheel. Red and green, blue and orange, yellow and violet (purple) are all complementary pairings.

Any value qualifies. Peach and navy? Complementary. Pink and light green? Complementary. The complements do not have to be used in the same proportion to qualify for color-scheme status. A whole lot of purple and a tiny bit of yellow is still a complementary color scheme. There are also some fancy versions of complementary color schemes: split complementary (a color plus the two colors on each side of its complement—a total of three colors) and double split complementary (the two colors lying on each side of two complementary colors—a total of four colors).

■ *Triadic colors* divide the color wheel into thirds. Purple, orange, and green are triadic colors, as are the primary colors—red, yellow, and blue—and their shades, burgundy, gold, and navy.

■ *Polychromatic* means "all colors" or "many colors." If you made a quilt of rainbow colors or a scrap quilt of muslin plus all the colors in your scrap bag, you would have a polychromatic quilt.

There are no rights and wrongs for color. But in my opinion, if what you're after is rich color, forget the first three palettes and work from the last three. Richness comes from using colors on opposite sides of the color wheel, or from using those all around it. There is nothing wrong with a blue-and-white quilt. But rich color is not what the quilt will be about. The impact will come from pattern—produced by value contrast.

Whether you choose to work with a limited range or the entire color wheel, vary the values. If you use greens, select several values. Avoid trying to match colors exactly. Mixing yellow-greens, pure greens, and blue-greens—call them avocado, kelly, and teal, if you like—can make a vastly more interesting combination than greens that are in the same family.

Add richness to your palette by jumping across the color wheel and including colors from the opposite side of the main (or theme) colors. You can make a quilt in everybody's favorites—red-violet, blue-violet, and purple (or how about magenta, delphinium, and teal)—and make it ever so much richer with a splash of yellow-orange (cantaloupe). Those favorite cool colors will still predominate, but jumping across the color wheel and adding a little warmth will enhance, enrich, and deepen the relationships among the hues. Think of oatmeal without a pinch of salt and a little brown sugar. Too one-dimensional, no?

Don't feel you need to use colors in the same proportion. A predominantly blue-and-purple quilt could be made richer and livelier with the addition of a little red-orange and just a splash of chartreuse—and still be predominantly blue and purple. Those accent colors could be a small part of a print that is primarily your theme color.

Most of us have color preferences and prejudices. Try your best to keep an open mind when it comes to choosing colors for your quilts. That harvest gold—out of vogue, and perhaps horrible on you when you wear it—could be just the thing to add depth and richness to the cobalt blue, royal purple, and red-violet fabrics you're putting together for your latest quilt.

The bottom line is this: If you work with color intuitively, throw away all these words and keep doing it that way. If you struggle with color, use the words, the theory, and the color schemes to help you make choices until you feel more comfortable working with color.

Put your hand over one group, then over the other. Which do you like better? Does the printed strip alone improve the blue-and-purple group?

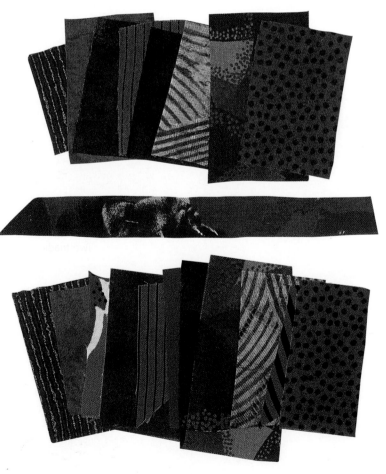

Value

Consider value—the lightness or darkness of a color—as a design element. *Value defines a composition.* Light, dark, and middle values allow us to see, or "read," a design. Consider the quilt blocks on this page. Each block is exactly the same—the Ohio Star. Because the darks and lights are placed differently, we read the designs differently.

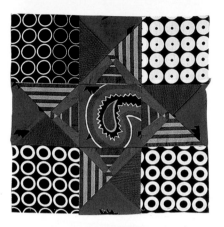

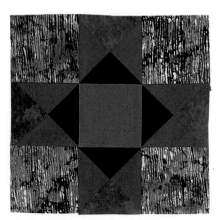

Each of these identically pieced Ohio Star blocks appears different because of different value placement.

Contrast refers to degrees of difference. *High contrast* means there is a lot of difference between values. *Low contrast* means there is little difference between values.

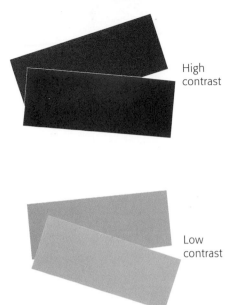

High contrast

Low contrast

Quilts with high contrast are usually dramatic; those with low contrast are usually more mellow. Some degree of contrast is necessary in order for you to see a composition. To help you see the values in a composition, try the following:

- ■ Squint—it's probably the most common way to check the value in a piece. When we squint, our eyelashes come together, reducing the light allowed into our eyes, restricting the amount of color we can perceive. We see lights, mediums, and darks more than colors, enabling us to evaluate a design based on its value.
- ■ Turn off the lights in your studio at dusk. If there is enough light to see shape, but not enough light to see color, you can read the value arrangement.
- ■ Use a reducing glass, which looks like a magnifying glass but makes objects appear smaller instead of larger. Looking through a camera's viewfinder, the wrong end of binoculars, or door peepholes also helps your work appear distant.
- ■ Take a Polaroid of your quilt-in-progress to get a new perspective. The photo reduces the image and diminishes the intensity of the colors, making it easier to see value.

Rembrandt van Rijn (1606–1669). *Aristotle Contemplating a Bust of Homer.* In this painting, Rembrandt employed wonderful, dramatic composition in darks and lights. (All rights reserved, The Metropolitan Museum of Art, New York, New York.)

When Rembrandt's *Aristotle Contemplating a Bust of Homer* is shown out of focus, we can see the composition clearly without the distraction of details or subject matter.

When I was a college freshman majoring in art, the teacher of my Basic Drawing course drummed good composition into the class by projecting out-of-focus slides of works painted by the masters. For painting after painting, we were asked to draw the arrangement of blurred areas of darks, lights, and mediums. Without being distracted by the subject matter or details, we drew value combinations until we internalized an understanding of good composition.

One of the lessons I learned in this process is that value defines a composition. Another, of course, is that if you want to study great composition, study Rembrandt!

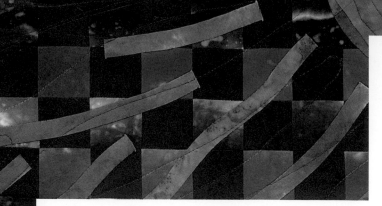

The quilt shown below came to me in a round-robin rotation. A traditional medallion-style quilt, it was a succession of borders added to an initial center block. I was the last of six people to add to the quilt. Although the scale was somewhat varied, the quilt lacked sparkling, little pieces to spice up the large and medium spaces. I solved this design problem by using small-scale half-square triangles in the final border.

Scale

Scale refers to the sizes and size relationships of a composition's parts. Most quilters are used to thinking about scale as the nature of a printed fabric—small-scale or large-scale florals, for example.

A quilt made only of tiny prints can look boring. A mix of large, medium, and small prints; open and dense prints; regular and random prints; and stripes, plaids, and polka dots is varied and interesting. Look at Reynola Pakusich's quilt "Earth" on page 54. Imagine it without the striped fabric. Wouldn't you agree that the impact would be diminished?

Sometimes, even when you choose fabrics with variety of value, color, and scale in mind, they still don't work well together. Ask yourself if the "flavor" is wrong. Chintz cabbage roses and a coordinating stripe may not be the right companions to a Mickey Mouse print—even if the color, value, and scale work according to all the rules. The prints seem to come from different planets.

There are other ways to vary the scale in a quilt. In the simplest terms, most good compositions have big spaces, medium spaces, and small spaces. A variety of sizes creates more visually satisfying scale relationships.

Prints of different scales

The Rose by Julia Zgliniec, Carolyn Maruggi, Dianne Ferguson, June Huntridge, Sally Ambrose, and Lorraine Torrence; machine quilted by Julia Zgliniec, 1997, Poway, California, 46" x 46". The outer border adds the small-scale pieces this quilt needed, and reintroduces white to the quilt. (Collection of Julia Zgliniec)

Look at the two quilt blocks below. Which is more interesting? Most of us would say the feathered eight-pointed star is more interesting than the simple eight-pointed star. But why? Don't even be tempted to say, "because the feathered star was harder" or " it took more skill" or "it took more time." These are not visual judgments. The reason the feathered star is more interesting is that there is more variety of scale. It has big spaces, medium spaces, and small spaces.

As you look at the quilts in this book, identify the big spaces, medium spaces, and small spaces in each. Remember that background, blank, or negative space is a legitimate, even important, design element. If you don't want to fill in a large space with a solid piece of fabric, consider using a subtle, visually textured print or an area pieced of fabrics close in color and value, which your eye will combine and "read" as one space.

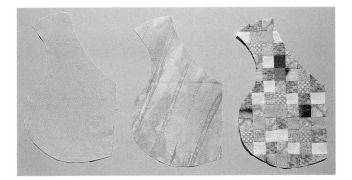

The same shape in a solid color, a subtly textured print, and a pieced unit, using close values. In a quilt, all three examples would function as a single light shape, but the second two would provide different degrees of visual texture.

Using a different vocabulary, Charles Smith, one of my art professors, constantly spoke of the need for "dominant, subdominant, and subordinate" elements in a composition. Obviously, these words do not apply exclusively to size. A small, bright yellow square in a large field of navy blue or black will be a dominant element, a focal point,

and not because of its size but because of its intensity in the context of its surroundings.

However we articulate it, we usually need to vary the scale, size, or emphasis of the units in our quilts to avoid either confusion or monotony. Look at the flower arrangement below. Notice the variation in the scale of the blossoms. Delicate, lacy flowers combine with bulky, dense ones. Tall, slender stems contrast with middle-sized clusters of bell-shaped flowers. The variety in scale increases the interest and rich exuberance of the bouquet.

In ikebana, the art of Japanese flower arranging, there are always three major stems in the arrangements. One is tall, one is of medium height, and one is low, often nearly horizontal. These three stems have symbolic meaning, but from a purely abstract design standpoint, they offer the variety of dominant, subdominant, and subordinate; large, medium, and small; major, minor, and focal; or whichever words seem most appropriate to describe the different role each part plays.

Balance

The arrangement of parts in a piece of art is the *composition*. The areas, the lines, the darks and lights that define them, the placement of color, the relative sizes of the different parts—all these ingredients must come together in a way that provides visual balance. Not surprisingly, our perception of balance is influenced most directly by the physical principle of gravity. We are most satisfied when there is equality (not always sameness) in the visual weight of parts on different sides of a piece of art. There are different types of balance that artists—and quilters—use to satisfy viewers.

Symmetrical Balance

Symmetrical balance is the type with which quilters are most familiar. Symmetrical balance implies a sameness on two or four sides of a four-sided quilt. How many quilts have you made using the one block in a grid arrangement that is the same left and right, top and bottom?

If the left half of your quilt is a repeat of the right half, the quilt is balanced symmetrically. If the left half is a mirror image of the right, it's balanced symmetrically. If you could rotate a quarter of the quilt one-quarter turn, then rotate it again and again without changing the overall design, the quilt is balanced symmetrically.

Notice that Jason Yenter's "Blue Horizon" is symmetrically balanced on a vertical axis. If you were to position a mirror along the vertical center line, you could

Blue Horizon by Jason Yenter, 1992, Seattle, Washington, 72" x 72". This quilt shows symmetrical balance on a vertical axis. Also notice the variety of scale: big spaces, medium spaces, and small spaces.

Scrappy Star, pieced by Nancy J. Martin, 1994, Woodinville, Washington, 32" x 32"; quilted by Donna K. Gundlach, Olympia, Washington. In this symmetrically balanced design, each quarter of the quilt could be rotated 90° and the composition would look the same. (Collection of Martingale & Company)

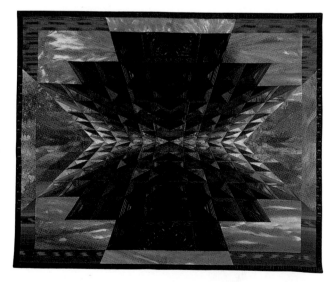

Ancient Directions by Alison Goss, 1991, Durango, Colorado, 80" x 67". Alison's quilt is symmetrical on both the horizontal and vertical axes. (Collection of The Museum of the American Quilter's Society, Paducah, Kentucky. Photo by Richard Walker, courtesy of the American Quilter's Society.)

see how the entire quilt looks. Tiny details that are different on the two sides do not keep the piece from being symmetrical.

Alison Goss's "Ancient Directions" is also a symmetrical quilt. Our first impression is that it is symmetrical on a horizontal axis, because the horizontal midpoint is so dominant. But the quilt is actually symmetrical on both its horizontal and vertical axes.

Symmetrical quilts are balanced by their very nature. The left is as visually "heavy" as the right, and often the top is as visually heavy as the bottom. A good reference on the many types of symmetry and how you can use them in quiltmaking is Ruth B. McDowell's *Symmetry: A Design System for Quiltmakers* (C&T Publishing, 1994).

Radial Balance

If equal parts of a composition are arranged in a circle, that is, in wedges, the composition is said to have *radial balance*. A true eight-pointed star composition or a single kaleidoscopic image is balanced radially.

Dawn Splendor by Nancy Ann Sobel, 1991, Brooktondale, New York, 94" x 94". This lovely quilt, an American Quilter's Society award winner, displays radial balance, a composition based on a circle. (Collection of the Museum of the American Quilter's Society, Paducah, Kentucky. Photo by Richard Walker, courtesy of the American Quilter's Society.)

Paula Nadelstern's kaleidoscopic images have radial balance. When she scatters them in a seemingly random way across the surface of the quilt, she uses value, color, and placement to achieve asymmetrical balance in the overall composition.

Detail of *Caribbean Blues*. Paula's kaleidoscopic images show radial balance.

Kaleidoscope XVII: Caribbean Blues by Paula Nadelstern, 1997, Bronx, New York, 66" x 71". Although the individual kaleidoscopic images are radially balanced, the composition of this entire quilt is asymmetrical. (Photo by Karen Bell)

Asymmetrical Balance

Asymmetrical balance is achieved when the parts are not the same on different sides of a quilt, but there is balance. This type of balance is accomplished the way two or three children on a teeter-totter are balanced by one adult. Achieving asymmetrical balance takes more skill and practice than symmetrical balance. Go back to the Rembrandt painting on page 11. It's a wonderful example of a successful asymmetrical composition.

Michael James's quilt "Horizontal Zag" is an exquisite example of asymmetrical balance. The dark and light areas are not the same on either side but are balanced in weight. The dark rectangle in the center right serves as a focal point that draws the eye first. Then the eye moves to the other darks, seeking similarity. The light area in the upper left is beautifully balanced by the other, smaller light areas. Strong diagonal movement, provided by the strips from lower left to upper right, is counterbalanced by wavy perpendicular lines. The darkening upper left corner, as well as the yellow-striped element in that corner, relate to areas on the other side of the strong light-to-dark diagonal.

Horizontal Zag by Michael James, 1988, Somerset Village, Massachusetts, 80" x 40". This quilt displays asymmetrical balance, being different from top to bottom and left to right. It remains perfectly balanced because of the placement of the darks and lights and the distribution of color. (Photo by James Beards)

Night Travel in the Mountains of Hakone by Hiroshige (1797–1858), 8⅞" x 13½", 1855. Asymmetry has been the composition of choice for nearly all traditional Japanese artists. (Courtesy of Carolyn Staley Fine Prints, Seattle, Washington)

Crystallographic Balance

Crystallographic balance, or balance without focal point, is a type of balance we encounter when the visual weight is the same all over. Ellen Oppenheimer's technical tour de force "Ari's Maze" is an example. No part is any stronger or more important than any other part.

Meiny Vermaas-van der Heide employed crystallographic balance in "Earth Quilt #56: Celebration of Life X." We find interest in visual texture and color, but no shape or area is dominant. The visual weight, produced mostly by value, is balanced consistently throughout.

Earth Quilt #56: Celebration of Life X by Meiny Vermaas-van der Heide, 1995, Tempe, Arizona, 59" x 51". Meiny's delicate pastel quilt is meant to "celebrate the fragility of new life." The absence of a focal point and the even texture are hallmarks of crystallographic balance.

Ari's Maze by Ellen Oppenheimer, 1994, Oakland, California, 46" x 46". Intricately matched stripes form an allover pattern that gives the quilt its crystallographic balance.

Unity

From Gestalt psychology we learn that people try to make sense out of what they see. We try to find relationships between visual elements. We try to unify the parts of what we see to make a related whole. When parts are too disparate, too unrelated, and the design of the piece does not hold together, we lose interest. If we want our quilts to capture our own interest and the interest of others, we need to learn how to unify them.

There are many strategies we can employ to achieve unity in our quilts.

Repetition

Repetition is used in all art forms. Repeating an image, a color, a shape, or a fabric gives it importance, creates a relationship, provides unity. We know units belong together if we see similarities among them.

Most often, repeated elements have more impact if they are used with some variation. The simple pieced blocks below are the same Attic Windows design. We see them as a unified whole because they are identical. They become more interesting when something in each block varies, in this case, the color.

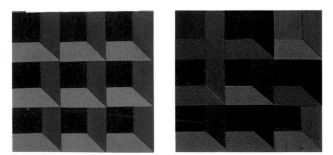

To create unity through repetition, repeat a shape, but in different sizes or colors; repeat a pattern, but in different fabrics; repeat a color, but in different values, intensities, or shapes.

Repetition is one of the most common methods of unifying any composition, whether it is a painting, a symphony, a poem, or a dance. Look at the quilts through-

out this book and identify where repetition is at work. In some of the quilts, complex, wiggly curves occur over and over. In others, a single shape repeats or a block design changes slightly as it shifts across the quilt surface.

In addition to unity, repetition provides impact. Nothing illustrates this better than New York's Radio City Music Hall Rockettes. One dancer making a gesture isn't extraordinary, but twenty-five dancers making the same gesture is compelling. Remember the Rockettes!

Grouping and Continuation

If you scatter a number of shapes randomly, and all the pieces are about the same distance apart, they may not appear to relate to each other. We won't "get" what is happening. It won't make sense.

Consider the shapes shown below. They don't seem to be related, do they? But the same shapes, rearranged in clusters, look unified. The unity is the result of proximity. Your eye reads a group as one unit.

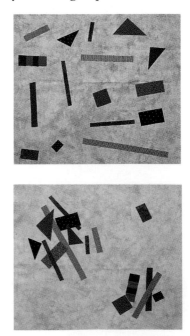

In addition to clustering, linear arrangements also help us see parts as a unified whole. In his book *Design Basics*, David Lauer calls this achieving unity by "continuation."

Shown below is a magnificent sampler quilt made by Phyllis Frye. Sampler quilts are not always the best examples of visual unity, but this is an extraordinary exception.

Most of us would instinctively stick to a color scheme when making diverse blocks for a sampler, which is what Mrs. Frye did, but she unified her design in other ways as well. All the block designs, which Mrs. Frye found in a patchwork calendar, are similar in weight—blocky, chunky, and compact. Look at the alternating block, set on point between each sampler block. The border-print stripe forms the **X** of each alternating block, linking to make a grid that holds the design together. The small squares in the border contrast with the bigger, chunkier shapes in the blocks, providing variation of scale. The small squares are repeated at the intersections of the sashing strips. Symmetrical balance. Unity provided by color, repetition, continuation. Interest provided by scale and pattern variation. Fabulous!

Design savvy is just as important in putting together a traditional quilt as it is in creating a unique, innovative quilt. Put the elements of good design to work for you when making quilts of any style. Combine them with other principles you'll discover as you continue to study design. Perhaps some people are born with artistic aptitude, but much of it can be learned. Practice, develop a visual vocabulary, and learn to see.

No Repeat Challenge by Phyllis Frye, 1992, Minden, Louisiana, 88" x 108". This traditional sampler quilt employs all the principles of great design. Mrs. Frye found the block designs in a calendar, but the wonderful setting is her own concoction. (Collection of James O. Frye; photo by David McCormick)

Design Approaches

This section outlines five approaches you can take to practice the design principles covered in pages 5–19. Some methods are spontaneous and easy, others are more analytical and will appeal to those of you who are left-brained artists.

These are not instructions for making specific quilts, but processes for increasing your ability to solve problems. Nearly every quilt we make presents a unique set of challenges. The more you know about design, color, and technique, the better equipped you will be to solve those problems when you come to them.

I prefer not to be limited by the boundaries of an exercise. The purpose of any exercise, after all, is to provide an impetus, an idea to get you started and a way to build your creative muscles. If, in the midst of the exercise, the work begins to pull you in another direction, make an executive decision. Determine if there is value in sticking to the "rules" for the time being (making a note of your bright ideas for future use) or if you'd rather go with the flow, whether or not it conforms to the limitations of the exercise. Sometimes a detour takes you on a more valuable journey.

Design Wall

If you don't already use a design wall, now is the time to start! A design wall is simply a large, flat, vertical surface (a wall, bulletin board, sheet of plywood, etc.) with a covering of thin batting, cotton flannel, felt, or other white, slightly fuzzy surface. The covering can be pinned, stapled, tacked, taped, glued, or otherwise attached to your design wall. Cotton fabrics stick to the fuzzy surface, so you don't have to pin pieces in place. (Remember how our kindergarten or Sunday-school teachers used flannel boards?) Silks, synthetics, and other filament or long-fiber fabrics may be too slick to stick to the design wall. Keep your pincushion handy for them.

Before you start working on your quilt, consider these thoughts:

■ Most people, probably including you, are better critics than inventors. Explore different options as you work on your design wall, without a predetermined idea of the outcome. Try something, then decide if you like it. Make visual decisions visually!

■ Be conscious of the movement of your eyes through the piece. If your eyes dart all over the work without finding a path, or go back and forth between unrelated items, you've probably created a disorganized piece. Try grouping elements in clusters or arranging them in lines to establish visual order. See pages 18–19.

■ Overlapping elements provides the illusion of depth, although it may make your composition more challenging to sew. Start by assuming you will be able to sew what you've designed. Try not to compromise design for the sake of technique. You'll usually find a way (or twelve ways!) to assemble your arrangement.

Collage Curves

If you are enamored of curves—as I am—you'll want to incorporate them into some of your quilts. Traditional methods involve piecing with carefully made templates or stitching appliqués. I prefer a more spontaneous approach—cutting shapes to size and covering the raw edges with machine-topstitched bias tape. Because this technique reminds me of the way I used to glue bits of paper to a background, I call it "Collage Curves."

The Collage-Curves method is a relatively quick and easy way to incorporate complex, free-flowing curves in a design. Using bias tape to finish the edges of the curves also adds line as a design element, something that doesn't show up in a lot of quilts.

Developing the Design

I usually begin by sketching a design on paper. Practice making loose, curvy lines. The looser your wrist and elbow as you draw, the more graceful your curves will be.

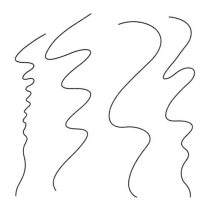

Designing on paper allows you to see several ideas without worrying about wasting materials or time. Remember, each sketch doesn't have to be The Masterpiece. Think of it as visual brainstorming. After several attempts—or maybe even a whole sketchbook of attempts—you'll probably find one or two that you like and want to develop into quilts. Perhaps you'll want to combine a particularly lovely squiggle from one sketch with the solidly balanced composition of another. Vary the scale of spaces, repeat visual elements—but with

variety—and color in darks and lights with a pencil to test the balance of the composition.

Assembling Tools and Materials

In addition to your design wall, sewing machine, iron, and ironing board, you need the following to make a Collage-Curves quilt:

- Preshrunk muslin or other light-colored, unprinted fabric the size you want your finished quilt to be
- Enough tissue paper to cover the entire piece of muslin
- Transparent tape for joining tissue-paper sheets
- Pencil or blue washout marker and a permanent-ink, fine-point black pen
- Straight pins, scissors, rotary-cutting equipment, hand-sewing needle, thread
- A collection of compatible fabrics
- Optional: Flexible curve and/or a French curve. If you have trouble drawing a graceful curve, consider using these tools. Relaxing your drawing arm may work just as well.

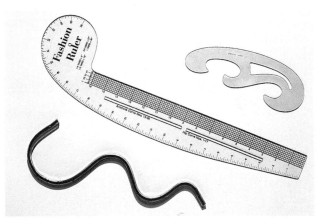

Flexible curve and French curves

Deciding how many fabrics you need and how much of each is not an exact science. Most quilters use a simple method: Buy a bunch of everything! (A "bunch" can be anything from one to three yards.)

Other methods require that you plan everything about your design. This is more economical than the Bunch-of-Everything yardage method but is a lot more time-consuming. You need to decide which fabrics to use and where to place them before you make the first cut. Then you must determine how much fabric each shape requires.

A comfortable compromise between the Bunch method and the Planning method is this: Decide how big you want your finished quilt or wall hanging to be, then determine how much fabric it would take to cover that area if you used only one fabric. Now double that amount. This will be a generous figure for the *combined total of all* the required fabrics. The proportion of each fabric to the total amount is up to you. You will, no doubt, use more of some fabrics than others. Realize that these yardage suggestions are approximate. Some of one fabric may be left over, or you may need more of another.

Preparing the Foundation

Once you have a design idea and have assembled your supplies, draw the design on a full-sized muslin foundation. I like to pin the muslin to my design wall to do the drawing. If you can't find fabric as large as the quilt you want to make, piece the foundation, placing the seams on the back when you draw.

Consider using an oversized foundation and drawing the quilt design in the center, with plenty of leftover space. You may feel the piece needs a border after you finish the main body of the quilt, and extra foundation fabric allows you to make a Collage-Curves border without having to add additional foundation fabric. You can always cut off any excess if your quilt looks complete without a border.

Transfer the design you drew on paper to the muslin foundation. I use a blue washout marker for this preliminary copying. Just freehanding it may work fine. If it's not exactly like the drawing on paper but looks okay—fine. If you feel the design loses something in the translation, try using an overhead projector (you can rent these at many camera-supply stores) or transfer the drawing using a proportional grid on both the paper drawing and the muslin foundation.

It's important to use a light-colored washout marker for the initial drawing on the muslin foundation. This way, you can correct mistakes by sponging them out, and lines won't show through light-value fabrics. As I draw, I often put hatch marks through the lines I don't want to use, then sponge them out after I've finished so I don't have to wait for the fabric to dry before I continue drawing.

When the drawing is complete, I trace it with a black permanent marker. Since these lines are positioned correctly, they'll lie under bias tape and won't show through light-value fabric.

For those of you who are concerned that the blue washout marker may harm your fabric, remove the muslin foundation from the wall and immerse it in water to remove the blue lines. Dry it in the dryer or iron it dry, then replace it on your design wall.

Cover the muslin foundation with tissue or tracing paper, pinning or taping the paper, if necessary, to make a large-enough piece. Trace the black-line drawing onto the tissue paper to make your pattern. Include the seam lines of the flip-and-sew areas (pages 24–25) on the tissue paper in case you decide to use the tissue as the foundation. If your piece is large, using a separate tissue-paper foundation may be more manageable than foundation piecing directly on muslin.

On the front of the tissue pattern, write your tentative fabric choice for each area. Not only does this tell you what to do with each pattern piece after you cut the shapes apart, but the writing on the pattern prevents you from turning over the pattern piece and cutting out a reversed shape.

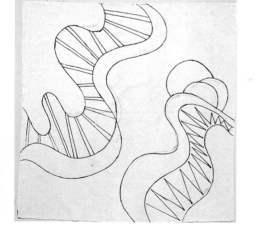

DESIGN DRAWN ON MUSLIN FOUNDATION

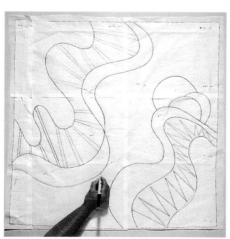

DESIGN TRACED WITH A BLACK PERMANENT MARKER

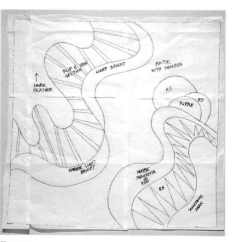

FABRIC CHOICES WRITTEN ON TISSUE PATTERN

Now, about those tentative fabric choices. Presumably, you've determined the value of the different pieces in your original drawing. Some people do well "winging it," mentally deciding what goes where. Others like to fill in the drawing with colored pencils. A few even photocopy and enlarge the drawing, then, using a gluestick, attach cut-to-scale fabric shapes. Auditioning fabrics (see photo below) is easiest for most of us.

Whichever way you like to work, make final judgments on fabric and color by pinning your cut-out selections in place on the foundation. (I always encourage quilters to make visual decisions visually, not intellectually.) We've all decided beforehand to use a certain fabric in a certain spot— for lots of good reasons—only to find that it's not right when it's in place. Don't hesitate to make a change at that point. In fact, never hesitate to change a piece after cutting it out or even after sewing it in place. Taking the time to make the change is worth it.

Cutting the Pieces

The beauty of this technique is that you don't need to worry about seam allowances. Cut the tissue-paper pattern into templates, pin the templates to the fabric, then cut out each piece. Don't be concerned with grain line; just cut the shapes whichever way the fabric looks best. Don't add a seam allowance, but if you cut slightly larger than the paper pattern, it's all right. The excess will only slightly overlap the piece next to it when you place it on the foundation.

As you cut each piece and place it on the foundation, check the fabric choices you made for the remaining pieces. It will become increasingly easy to know which fabrics are going to work based on what's already there. You can always hold up folded or even wadded-up fabrics to your partly filled foundation to test the relationship of one fabric to the others.

AUDITIONING FABRICS FOR COLOR AND VALUE PLACEMENT

Adding Flip-and-Sew Areas

If your design calls for small pieced or subdivided spaces, you can do some "flip-and-sew" foundation piecing. All of my Collage-Curves quilts include such areas. They provide visual texture and scale variety, and allow me to use more fabrics in the work. Including more fabrics usually translates to richness and interest, which is why scrap quilts are often more appealing than those with limited fabrics.

If your Collage-Curves quilt is small, you can do the flip-and-sew section directly on the muslin foundation.

1. If you haven't already done so, draw lines on the foundation or pattern to indicate the seams in the flip-and-sew areas. The lines you draw won't be the actual seam lines, as in most foundation piecing; they're there to help you align raw edges of fabric pieces at the desired angle.

2. Place a piece of fabric, right side up, over the first space on one end of the flip-and-sew section. Make sure the fabric covers the entire space, and its edge lines up with the first line on the foundation.

3. Choose the next piece of fabric and place it, wrong side up, on the first piece, matching raw edges as shown. (Make sure this piece is big enough to cover the second space after being sewn and flipped over.) Using a ¼"-wide seam allowance, sew the pieces together through the foundation, backstitching at the beginning and end of the seam. Do not sew beyond the boundary lines of the flip-and-sew section. Flip the fabric over the foundation and press.

4. Fold back the raw edge of the second fabric until the fold aligns with the next line on the foundation. Slip your scissors into the fold and cut.

5. Trim the pieces even with the boundaries of the flip-and-sew section.

6. Continue adding new pieces, repeating steps 3–5— sew, flip, press, trim—to complete the section.

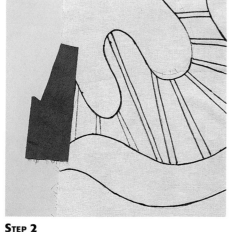

STEP 2

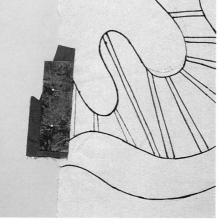

STEP 3

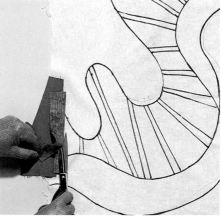

STEP 4

STEP 5

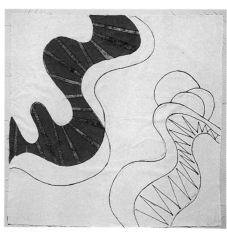

STEP 6

TIP

If you have flip-and-sew points or "teeth," draw them so the points stop ¼" from the edge of the section. This way, the bias strip covering the raw edges won't chop off the points.

Sew flip-and-sew points as in steps 1–6 on the facing page, but take care that the piece you are adding will cover the entire triangle when the piece is flipped.

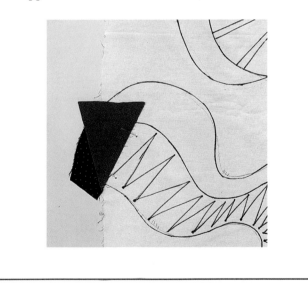

If your quilt is large and you don't want to handle the entire foundation as you flip and sew sections, piece a single section, using the tissue-paper pattern as the foundation. Follow steps 1–6, sewing through the tissue paper as you add each piece. Trim the fabric pieces even with the tissue-paper pattern as you sew them on—one at a time—or trim the entire length of both edges after completing the section.

After you finish sewing the pieces to the tissue foundation, tear off the paper and pin the pieced section in place on the muslin foundation.

TIP

It's also possible to strip piece or string piece fabrics to make large sections, then cut a shape from the pieced section, using the tissue-paper pattern as a guide.

Evaluating the Composition

When you've finished cutting sections and placing them on the muslin foundation, step back and take a look. If your work space doesn't allow you to get very far from your design wall, use a reducing glass or another tool to make the quilt look smaller. See page 11 of "Value" for a list of tools and techniques that reduce images.

Look for balance of value, color, and dominant, subdominant, and subordinate elements. Check for repetition of elements (with variety) and overall unity.

Attaching Pieces to the Foundation

If your quilt is small and manageable, and your machine feeds evenly (or if you have a walking foot), stitch the piece to the muslin foundation. If your quilt is large, I recommend hand basting around the edge of each piece for the flattest, smoothest results.

To machine stitch pieces to the muslin, use a zigzag stitch wide enough to catch the edge of each adjoining piece (on each side of the "seam"). If the raw edges of the pieces overlap slightly, you may be able to catch both edges with one straight stitch. If the edges are a bit too far apart to catch with one row of stitches or if your machine doesn't zigzag, straight stitch along each edge.

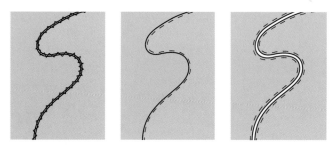

A common problem at this stage is pieces shifting on the muslin, which results in a surface that won't lie flat. Another problem can be an unevenly fed stitch—if the fabric layers move through the machine at different rates, the muslin foundation draws up and won't lie flat.

If you encounter these problems, lay your quilt on a smooth, flat surface. Making sure all pieces are pinned so they lie flat on the foundation, hand baste the edges of each piece to the muslin, using a straight basting stitch or overcast stitch.

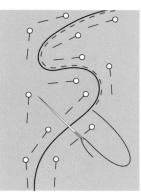

Baste non-overlapping edges with an overcast stitch.

Baste overlapping edges with a running stitch.

Whether you attach your pieces to the foundation with hand or machine stitches—straight stitch, zigzag, or overcast stitch—keep the stitches within a ⅜"-wide area where the pieces join. You want the bias strip that will cover the raw edges to cover the basting also. If the basting stitches extend beyond the bias strip, you'll need to remove them later.

Using Bias Tape

Covering raw edges with bias strips produces a clean, finished look and also adds linear elements to your design. Any fabric will achieve the first goal, but to produce additional lines in your quilt, you need to choose a color or value for the bias tape that will contrast with the fabrics on each side. Using the same fabric as one of the two you are joining produces a barely noticeable line and slightly enlarges the matching-fabric section.

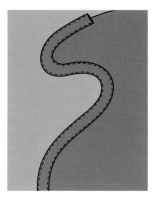

Contrasting bias

Matching bias

It's worth it to cut a few ½"-wide bias strips from the fabrics you are considering for bias tape. For a visual test, pin the strips in position over the raw edges of the curved pieces. Select the bias tape you like best for each seam covering.

Unless your fabric is wider than 45" (or 40" to 42" wide after it's preshrunk), the longest piece of bias tape you can make is about 60" long (the diagonal measurement of a 42" x 42" square). The tape may stretch a little as you make it, giving you a few extra inches. If your quilt is large, you may need to cover a seam that is longer than your tape. In this case, either piece the bias tape or look for places where the bias strip can be crossed by another, so you can start another strip under the crossover piece.

I don't recommend using packaged bias tapes. Often, the quality of the fabrics in commercial bias tapes is different from that of your quilt fabrics. I prefer to make my bias tapes from fabrics already represented in the quilt. Repeating the fabrics as bias tapes results in greater design unity.

However you make the bias tape, remember this: In the final analysis, the cool tools or slick tricks you use to achieve your goal probably won't change the way your quilt looks. Chances are, no one will be able to walk up to your quilt and observe, "Oh, she used the Pin-in-the-Ironing-Board trick to make her bias tape." What *does* change the look of your quilt is good design and good color.

Making Bias Tape

There are several ways to make bias tape. My favorite method doesn't require the purchase of anything special. It's the "Pin-in-the-Ironing-Board" trick, which I learned from a fellow teacher in 1989. (She couldn't remember who taught it to her so I can't credit its source.)

To do this technique, insert a pin in your ironing-board cover—perpendicular to the side of the ironing board—so it goes in, comes out, and goes in again. The interval between the spot where the pin first comes out and the second insertion point should equal the finished width of the bias tape you want to make—between ⅜" and ½".

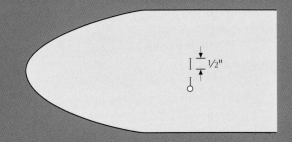

Cut the desired number of the longest-possible true-bias strips from the fabrics you want to use. (Cut true-bias strips at a 45° angle to the selvage edge of the fabric.) Slightly more than twice the width of the desired finished bias width works well—1" to 1⅛" wide. Fold under the long edges of the bias strip so they overlap, and insert the folded bias, raw edges up, under the pin on the ironing board.

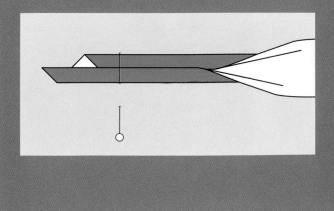

If you are right-handed, insert the folded bias from right to left as shown, and pull it with your left hand, passing it under the pin. Guide the bias strip with your right hand, making sure the folded edges stay overlapped in the center. If you are left-handed, reverse the direction in which you pull the tape.

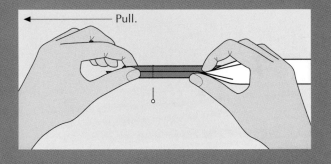

Pull the folded strip about 8" under the pin, release the tension slightly with your left hand, then press the strip. Set the iron aside, pull the strip another 8", release the tension, and press again. Repeat the pull-release-press cycle to finish each bias tape.

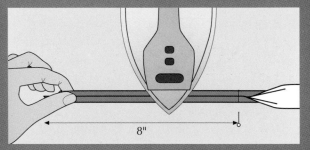

Be certain to include the "release" part of the cycle so you don't press the bias tape into a stretched position. A stretched-and-pressed tape may relax after you stitch it to your quilt, causing it to pucker.

Stitching the Bias Tape in Place

To topstitch the bias tape in place, I straight stitch along both edges with a thread that matches the tape. Use any light- to middle-value thread in your bobbin and change the color of the top thread as needed. If you can identify bias-tape sections that begin and end under other pieces, stitch those in place first. Trim the end of the piece you've sewn at the same angle as the bias strip that will cover it. Keep the raw edges of the sections under the center of the tape that covers them.

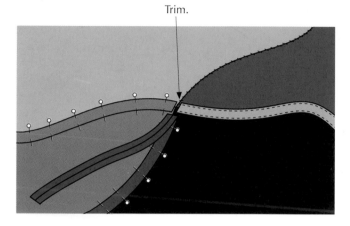

Trim.

If your bias lines curve around, over, and under each other in a complicated pattern, it's best to pin the various tapes in place before stitching to discover the best order in which to sew them.

If the end of one tape lies under another and you have already sewn the tape on top, stitch up to, but not across, the stitched tape. You could backstitch here, but I prefer to pull the threads through to the back and tie them. This is more attractive than backstitching and makes the stitching look as though it continues under the tape on top.

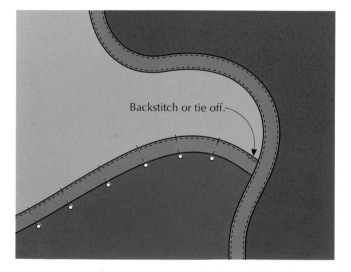

Backstitch or tie off.

Thorough steam pressing will set the stitches and make everything lie flat. If your quilt puckers after you stitch the bias tape in place, you can slit the muslin foundation from the back to release some of the bunching. The batting and backing will cover the slit.

Borders

Is your quilt complete without a border, or does it seem to lack something? I often finish my Collage-Curves quilts with only a binding, but I've added borders (even ones that included more bias-joined collage curves) to some. Find a more extensive discussion in "Borders," beginning on page 92.

Quilting Your Collage-Curves Quilt

Since you have lots of topstitching on it already, machine quilting is appropriate for a Collage-Curves quilt. If it seems fitting, I sometimes combine hand and machine quilting.

The muslin foundation is a permanent part of a Collage-Curves quilt, making an additional layer through which to quilt. If you are an enthusiastic hand quilter who relishes the idea of hand appliquéing the bias strips in place and then hand quilting the quilt, the additional thickness may prevent you from making stitches as tiny as you're accustomed to. You could opt for a larger stitch as a design element or cut the muslin foundation from the back of the quilt top, leaving only narrow muslin "ribbons" under the bias joinings.

■ *Auntie Maude's Flower* by Judy Robertson, 1997, Bow, Washington, 43" x 36". This lusciously colored quilt, created mostly from Judy's own hand-dyed fabric, is a great example of asymmetrical balance. Even though the red spiky areas in the upper left are large, they cover only about a third of the piece. The more numerous but smaller red-and-orange "teeth" cover a larger area. This rich complementary color scheme is rendered even richer by the mottled fabric.

■ *Nemo's Ecstasy* by Lorraine Torrence, 1997, Seattle, Washington, 42" x 45½". DYEnamic Fabrics and Designs produced the dark-blue-to-yellow-green hand-dyed fabric gradation used in the middle of the quilt. After I pieced the two checkerboard sections, I found the result too geometric and harsh for the undulating underwater effect I wanted. I painted over it with a light blue textile paint to bring the values closer together. If this had not satisfied me, I would have lifted out the section and substituted something else for this part of the quilt.

■ *Hale-Bopp* by Mary Cecilia Burton, 1997, Stanwood, Washington, 40" x 50". The color glows, the diagonal composition is nicely balanced, and Collage-Curves piecing shows dynamic movement.

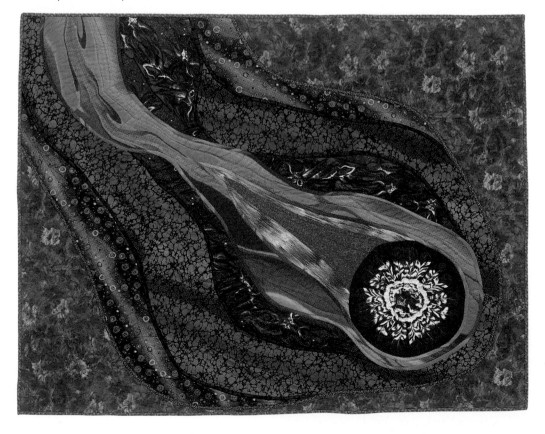

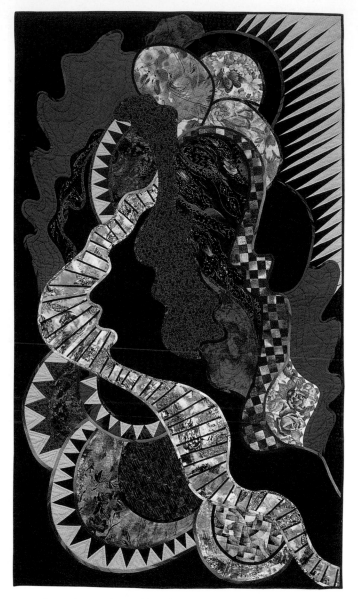

■ *Cosmic Confluence* by Lorraine Torrence, 1996, Seattle, Washington, 60½" x 68½". The large pink-orange piece was painted by Mickey Lawler of Skydyes. It perfectly suggests the magma-like surface of this heavenly body.

■ *Motion Pink Swirl* by Shirley Tyler, 1997, Lake Stevens, Washington, 39" x 68"; machine quilted by Shirley Tyler and Patsi Hanseth. Lots of flip-and-sew areas give this ambitious piece unity. The repetition of triangular shapes of different sizes and angles and the repeated checkerboard areas in different fabrics combine with the constant rhythm of the curvy lines. With all the spectacular activity, Shirley made sure there were some large, plain areas to provide contrast. Because of the quilt's size, Shirley hand appliquéd the bias strips to avoid the shifting she thought might occur under the presser foot of a machine.

■ *Leaf Fall* by Marty Kutz, 1996, Sedro Woolley, Washington, 22" x 28". Marty repeated the curving lines throughout the quilt.

■ *Confluence* by Louise Harris, 1997, Sedro Woolley, Washington, 35½" x 35". The topographical-maplike quality, suggesting the merging of rivers, is easy to produce with the Collage-Curves technique. Louise's exquisitely balanced composition and color choices make a harmonious whole.

■ *Riverscape* by Lorraine Torrence, 1997, Seattle, Washington, 55" x 68¾". The color and value placement in the border balances this piece. The bias tape not only covers raw edges; the intertwining lines form an integral part of the design.

■ *Moonlight Dragon* by Lorraine Torrence, 1995, Seattle, Washington, 38" x 26". The large light-value area was too bland when filled with one piece of solid fabric, so I pieced several fabrics that were close in value and color to provide visual texture.

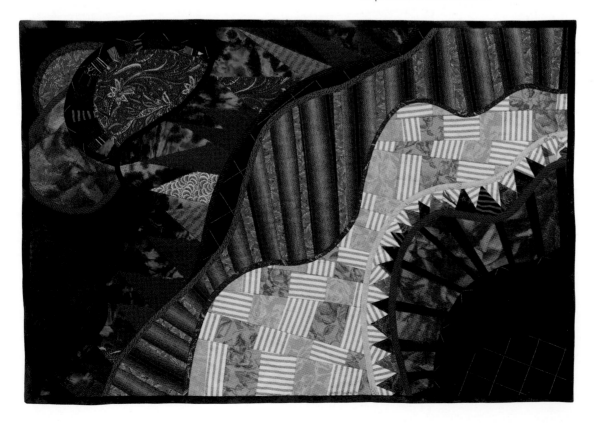

Slash and Sew

Perhaps you want to place shapes on an expanse of fabric but don't want to appliqué them. Piecing is quicker, and it keeps lines crisp and points sharp.

Assembling Tools and Materials

In addition to your design wall, sewing machine, iron, and ironing board, you need:

- Background fabric that is two to three inches bigger all around than the piece you want to make, plus about ½ yard extra for extensions. Allow even more if you want to use the fabric in the borders. (For a very small quilt, such as our step-by-step sample, an extra ¼ yard will be ample.) I suggest starting with a small background, such as 24" x 30", for your first attempt. (See "A Word About Backgrounds" at right for hints on fabric selection.)
- 8 to 10 fabrics, each approximately 6" x 12", for the floating elements. Most pieces should contrast with the background.
- Rotary cutter, large cutting mat, 24"- long acrylic ruler and a shorter ruler, 12" to 14" long
- Metal yardstick or extra-long straightedge
- Chalk marker, pins, scissors

A Word About Backgrounds

When choosing a background fabric, consider pattern, value, and color. If your background is busy or heavily patterned, it will be difficult to see the floating elements. Floating elements with low contrast provide subtle shapes that barely emerge from the background. Low-contrast shapes can be interesting, but don't rely on them exclusively. Remember—value defines a composition.

Solid, low-contrast, and lightly mottled or subtly patterned backgrounds, such as those below left, show inserted designs more clearly. You can use stripes and other directional fabrics for backgrounds, but keep them delicate.

Preparing Floating Design Elements

Simple shapes such as strips, squares, triangles, and rectangles are all logical candidates for setting into a background. Another option is to strip piece fabrics first, then cut strips, squares, and other shapes from the strip set to make pieced floating shapes.

More complex shapes like stars, cubes, miniature block designs, and curves can also be set into a background. You simply add background-fabric extensions to expand the complex shapes into simple ones.

Gather many different cut shapes and pieced elements before going to your design wall. Precut shapes allow you to work quickly and spontaneously. Of course, you may not use everything you cut, and you may need to stop and cut more. Guard against the temptation to use all the pieces you made just because you took the time to make them. If they don't work in the design, don't use them.

Vary the sizes and shapes of the elements, but repeat some of the fabrics and shapes within that variety. For instance, if you cut a yellow triangle, use the yellow somewhere else, but in a different size and perhaps a different shape. If you use squares, don't make them all the same size. Repetition is a unifying principle, but variety is engaging.

Planning Your Quilt

Review "Design Principles" on pages 5–19 before you start. In addition, consider the following:

- Keep the principles of grouping and continuation (pages 18–19) in mind. If you surround all your floating shapes with the same amount of negative space, the design will probably be weak, without pathways for the eye to follow. Cluster elements or arrange them in a line for unity.
- Overlap and stack shapes to create the illusion of depth. Try to design without worrying about how you'll stitch.

Since the slash-and-sew technique is easier to explain if the instructions address a specific layout, I'll go through the steps needed to make the quilt shown at right.

1. From the 8 to 10 pieces of fabric, cut strips in a variety of widths (¾" to 2½" wide) and about 12" long. Sew enough strips together to make 2 strip sets, each about 10" x 12". Sew the strips in a different order in each set.
2. Cut several segments in various widths (¾" to 1¼" wide) from the strip sets. Make perpendicular cuts for a few segments and diagonal cuts for others. Cut additional shapes from the fabrics you used to make the strip sets, varying the sizes and shapes.
3. Put the background fabric on the design wall. Place cut shapes on the background, arranging and rearranging until you arrive at a composition you like.
4. Pin the pieces in place on the background fabric without also pinning them to the design wall.

Note: Remember, these cut shapes will be smaller by ¼" all the way around after you sew them into the quilt. If you have trouble visualizing your pieces this small, bite the bullet and cut them to finished size. When your layout is finished, replace all the cut pieces with duplicates cut ¼" larger all around. Okay, so you've wasted a little fabric—it's worth it if it helps you visualize the design. ■

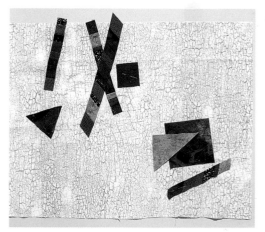

Cutting the Quilt into Sections

1. Now you're ready to start slashing. Take your background fabric—with the design pieces pinned in place—to your cutting mat. Move a yardstick across the background to find a straight line that crosses the quilt top from edge to edge but does not run into any floating shapes.

   Note: There's usually more than one spot for a continuous line across the quilt. This line will be a seam eventually, and therefore a subtle design line, so choose the option that makes the most interesting design element. In an asymmetrical design, a diagonal seam might be more interesting than a vertical one through the middle of the quilt.

   Occasionally—although rarely—you won't find an uninterrupted line that crosses a quilt or section. Try moving one of the pieces slightly to see if you can find a straight line. If you compromise the design by doing this, don't. Settle for a bent line, which will require a set-in seam.

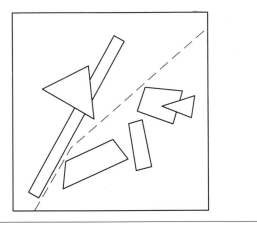

2. Using your rotary cutter, cut on the line. Make sure it's a straight cut—use a metal yardstick or a longer straightedge if your line is longer than your cutting ruler. (If the line is longer than the longest cutting edge you have, mark the line first, then make the cut by moving the ruler along the marked cutting line.) Separate the sections of the quilt top.

   Note: If you need to remove a few pins so your ruler will lie flat on the quilt surface, do so, but replace them after you've made the cut. A chalk mark or two across the cutting line will help you match the edges when you sew the two halves back together. ⸻⬛

3. Replace the right side on the design wall. At the cutting mat, find another line that will separate the left section into smaller, simpler parts. A good dividing line in this section is shown in the middle photo below.

4. Make the cut and add chalk hatch marks before you separate the pieces.

Assembling the Left Side

1. You need to cut this section again, between the two shapes. If you make the cut at the bottom of the strip, you won't need to add an extension of background fabric to it.

2. To insert the strip in the upper section, you need to cut the background apart, directly under the center of the strip. I place the edge of my cutting ruler down the middle of the strip and carefully pull the strip out from under the ruler.

CUTTING THE QUILT INTO SECTIONS: STEP 2

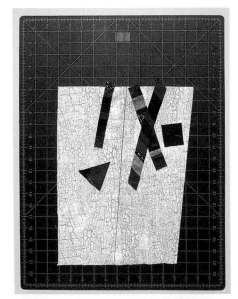

CUTTING THE QUILT INTO SECTIONS: STEP 3

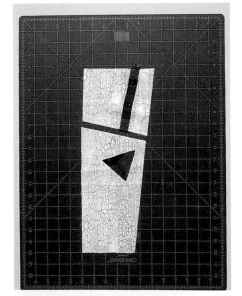

ASSEMBLING THE LEFT SIDE: STEP 1

TIP:

To pull a shape from under the right edge of a cutting ruler without disturbing the background and any other floating pieces, press hard on the left edge of the ruler. The right side will lift up enough to allow you to pull a shape from under it.

3. Make the cut and reposition the strip between the two sections.

4. Sew the two background sections to the strip and press. Set this completed section aside, or replace it on your design wall to keep track of its position and orientation.

5. For the lower section with the triangle, there are two options. A triangle can be inset either as a strip with extensions on two sides (A), or as part of a wedge shape (B). The dotted lines in the illustrations represent the options for seam lines.

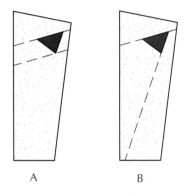

A   B

I'll choose option B, since I prefer the way it looks. (We'll extend a shape into a strip—option A—later.) Align a ruler with the upper edge of the triangle and make a rotary cut. Set aside the top piece of background. Repeat to cut the background along the right side of the triangle.

6. The floating triangle now sits on top of a triangle of background fabric. Align the ½" mark on your rotary ruler with the left edge of the floating triangle, and carefully pull it out.

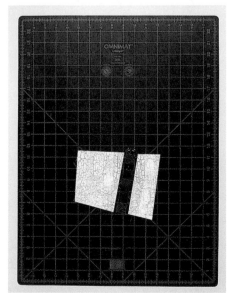

ASSEMBLING THE LEFT SIDE: STEP 3

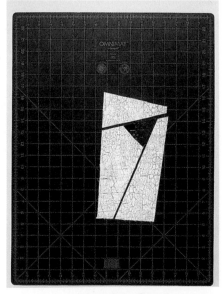

ASSEMBLING THE LEFT SIDE: STEP 5

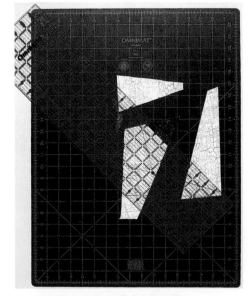

ASSEMBLING THE LEFT SIDE: STEP 6

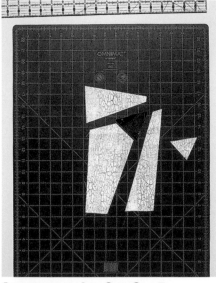

ASSEMBLING THE LEFT SIDE: STEP 7

ASSEMBLING THE LEFT SIDE: STEP 8

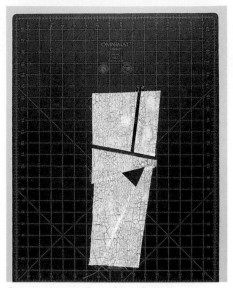

ASSEMBLING THE LEFT SIDE: STEP 9

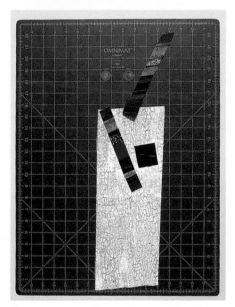

ASSEMBLING THE MIDDLE SECTION: STEP 1

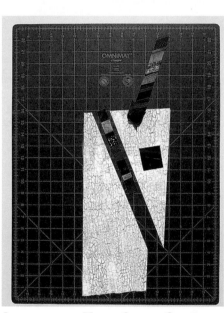

ASSEMBLING THE MIDDLE SECTION: STEP 3

ASSEMBLING THE MIDDLE SECTION: STEP 4

7. Cut the background fabric along the edge of the ruler. Discard the background triangle. Sew the floating triangle to the background piece.

8. If necessary, trim the edges of the new combination.

9. Add the background piece you removed in step 5, then add the top left section with the inlaid strip from step 4. Trim the edges as necessary. Voilà! The left side of the quilt is finished!

Assembling the Middle Section

The middle section includes a crossover strip, a strip that covers another. You must first piece the underneath strip into the background, then make the cut for the top strip.

1. Pin the top strip in place at its upper end and lift the lower part up and out of the way.

2. Place a ruler along the center of the crossunder strip, carefully remove the strip, then cut the background apart as you did in step 2 of "Assembling the Left Side" on page 34.

3. Place the crossunder strip between the two background pieces. This strip needs a background-fabric extension to reach the end of the cut.

4. From the extra ¼ to ½ yard of background fabric, cut a strip a little wider than the crossunder strip. In the sample, the strip is ¾" wide, so cut a 1"-wide extension. Cut the ends of the strip and the extension at matching angles, sew them together, then press. Trim

the extension to the same width as the strip to be inlaid.

5. At this point, it is oh-so-tempting to sew the strip into the background. But first you have to insert the square that floats to the right. Whichever way you add extensions to this square, the seams will interfere with the seams of the inlaid crossunder strip, so you must insert the square before sewing the strip to the background. The dotted lines in the illustration represent the extension seams.

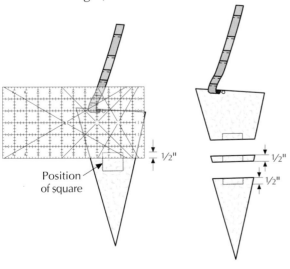

6. Mark the position of the square with chalk. Remove the square. Align the ½" mark on your ruler with one edge of the chalk-marked square, and make a rotary cut along the ruler's edge. Align the ½" mark on the ruler with the edge you just cut, and cut again. (See the Note at right).

Note: The square in the example is 1" x 1" finished, 1½" x 1½" cut. Whenever a floating shape is more than ½" wide (finished), you must remove part of the background behind it in order to maintain the shape's position on the background. If you don't remove the background behind the piece, you'll change the spacing of the floating pieces and the design of the quilt.

Original design · Insertion without removing background strip; the spacing doesn't match the original design. · Insertion after removing background strip; the spacing matches the original design.

The only time you don't have to remove background is when the floating piece is ½" wide (finished), because that piece is just wide enough to allow ¼"-wide seam allowances for the inserted strip and the background underneath. The background spacing will remain unchanged after you slash and insert. (When inserting a ¾"-wide strip—¼" wide finished— cut the background under the center of the strip and insert the strip. In this case, the background will move ¼" closer together.)

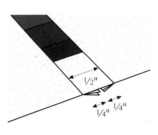

The rule for this situation is: *From the background, remove an amount that is 1" less than the floating shape's cut width.* In the sample, the cut size of the 1" finished square is 1½": 1½" - 1" = ½". You must remove ½" from the background. If the square or strip were 2" wide finished and 2½" wide cut, you would remove 1½" from the background fabric.

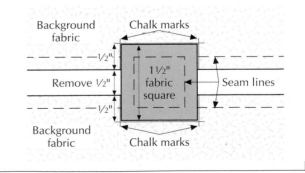

7. Add extensions to the square, trim to clean up the edges, then sew the pieced strip into the background, centering the square between the chalk marks. Press, then clean up the edges.

8. Sew the three sections together. Press, then trim to clean up the edges.

9. Replace the crossover strip and place an edge of the ruler along the center of the strip. Remove the strip and cut. (Yes—cut right through what you just pieced!) Remember to remove background fabric (and parts of any inset shapes sewn to the background) if the strip is wider than ½" finished (1" cut).

10. Add an extension to the crossover strip, press, then trim to clean up the edges. Sew the strip to one side of the background.

11. To make sure the other half of the strip is properly placed and looks as though it continues in a straight line under the crossover strip, mark the points that need to match on the back of the fabric.

12. Place the pieces right sides together, pinning at the matching points, and stitch, using a scant ¼"-wide seam allowance. Press, then trim to clean up the edges. The center section is complete!

> **TIP:**
> I like to machine baste a short seam along the critical area, then check the front to see if the pieces line up correctly. If they don't, I remove the stitches, make adjustments, and repeat until it looks right. Then I stitch the entire seam, using a regular stitch length.

Assembling the Right Side

1. The right side has an overlap (a bit of a challenge) and a simple strip (a piece of cake). Mark the strip placement on the background with chalk, cut the background under the center of the strip, then add extensions to the strip. Press and trim to clean up the edges.

2. Before sewing the strip in place, you must inset the triangle that overlaps the square. To make the piecing possibilities easier to analyze, trace complex groupings onto paper, then draw lines where you'll slash.

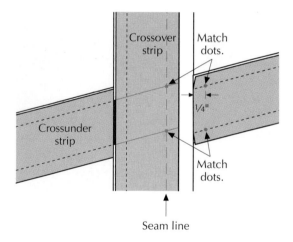

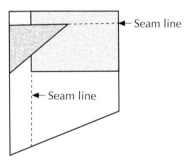

ASSEMBLING THE MIDDLE SECTION: STEP 7

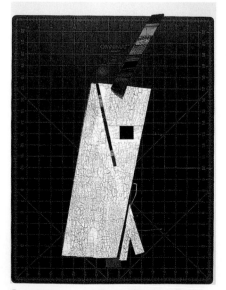

ASSEMBLING THE MIDDLE SECTION: STEP 8

ASSEMBLING THE MIDDLE SECTION: STEP 9

3. Always break complex shapes into simple ones. On your drawing, make a line that extends all the way across the unit—in this case, the line across the top of the triangle.

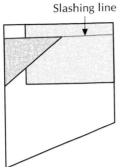

Slashing line

4. Find a cutting line that goes all the way across the lower section; here, it's along the long side of the triangle.

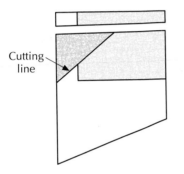

Cutting line

5. Continue to break the piece apart, looking for lines that extend all the way across the remaining piece. Here's how this "overlap" section breaks down:

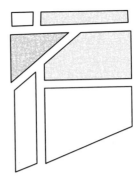

6. Cut new pieces from the same fabrics as the original floating shapes, *adding seam allowances as you cut*. Sew the pieced shapes together, using the illustration below as a guide.

Assembly order

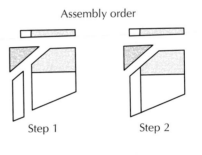

Step 1   Step 2

   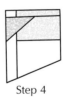

Step 3   Step 4

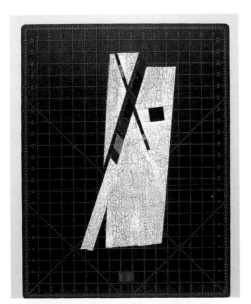

ASSEMBLING THE MIDDLE SECTION: STEP 10

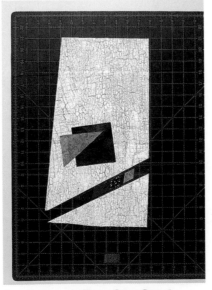

ASSEMBLING THE RIGHT SIDE: STEP 1

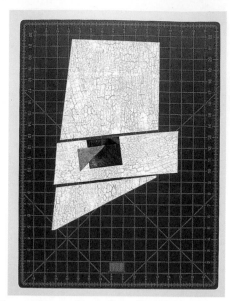

ASSEMBLING THE RIGHT SIDE: STEP 7

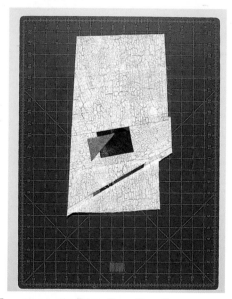

ASSEMBLING THE RIGHT SIDE: STEP 8

ASSEMBLING THE RIGHT SIDE: STEP 9

7. Insert the pieced section into the background.

8. Add the extended strip made in step 1 and the corner background triangle to the bottom of the piece. Press; then clean up the edges to complete the right section of the quilt top.

9. Sew all three sections together and clean up the edges. Border it as you wish.

Learning to Analyze a Design

An easy way to identify the best cutting and construction order for a quilt is to sketch the layout on paper, then draw in possible seam lines. Here is a design and one possible construction solution:

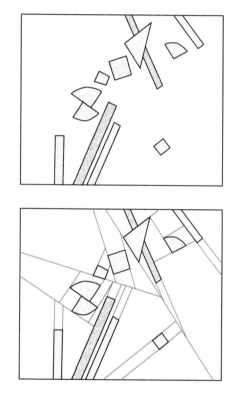

After you've drawn the lines, look for lines that go all the way across the existing piece, and mentally take it apart there. If you can't find any, draw them in! Continue to break down each remaining section, looking for lines that extend from edge to edge. Keep breaking down the design into the simplest parts. Remember that the first line you identify as going all the way across is the last line you sew when you put it all together.

I often liken this technique to playing chess: you have to think several moves ahead. I love staying engaged throughout the process.

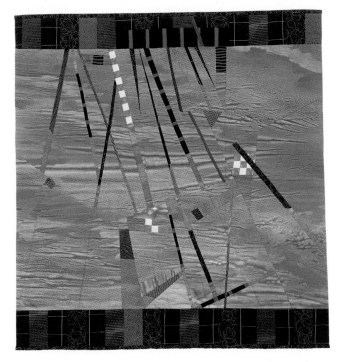

■ *Acid Rain* by Lorraine Torrence, 1996, Seattle, Washington, 34" x 36". Mickey Lawler's hand-painted fabric was almost too variegated to work as a slash-and-sew background. I had only one yard, and the small piece I set aside didn't provide me with many choices for cutting extensions. I like the ambiguous effect the extensions produce—as if the atmosphere is almost thick enough to be solid.

■ *Chance of Scattered Showers* by Sue Pelton, 1997, Seattle, Washington, 20" x 36½". Crisscrossing "rain" strips turn into a colorful garden at the lower edge of the quilt, and a raindrop sparkle of beads provides textural interest.

■ *Volcano Rain* by Lorraine Torrence, 1997, Seattle, Washington, 49¼" x 44". A beautiful piece of Judy Robertson's hand-dyed fabric provides the background for this slash-and-sew quilt. The variations in the fabric become players in the composition, along with the scattered floating pieces. I never hesitate to leave large, open spaces in a composition. Sometimes less is more.

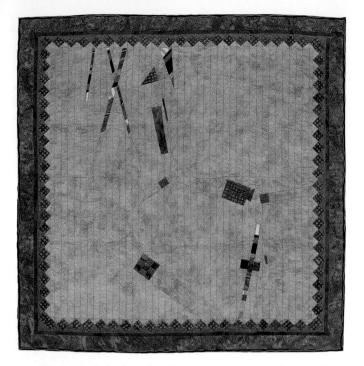

■*Santa Fe* by Lorraine Torrence, 1997, Seattle, Washington, 39½" x 41"; quilted by Gretchen Engle. Quilts with free-floating shapes often need structured, predictable borders. Using the background fabric on the inner edge of a pieced border brings it into the interior.

■*Three Fans Two* (below) by Laura Munson Reinstatler, 1988, Mill Creek, Washington, 72" x 48". Laura pieced the fans first, then arranged them. Using tracing-paper patterns as templates, she added some of the vertical strips before setting the fans into the background, which required careful planning!

■*Autumn Interlude* (above) by Christina Wright, 1997, Woodinville, Washington, 32" x 57". This beautiful border contains variations of shapes used in the interior. The background fabric is plain enough to allow us to focus on the floating shapes but textured enough to be interesting.

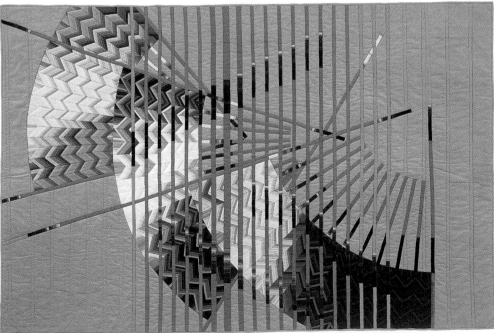

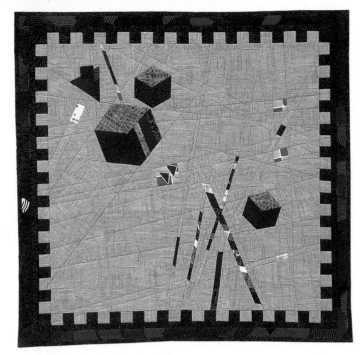

■ *Toys for Baby Astronauts* by Lorraine Torrence, 1997, Seattle, Washington, 30¼" x 30¼". Two sizes of Tumbling Blocks provide variety. A narrow strip in the upper left corner repeats the linear elements in the lower right. You won't see as much unity in the design if you cover the little strip in the upper left. Put your finger over the cube in the lower right quadrant and see how the piece goes off balance in the same way.

■ *Clockwise, Counterclockwise* by Kerry I. Smith, 1997, Bainbridge Island, Washington, 29" x 36". Kerry worked with colors and fabrics she loves, repeating the checkerboard element with variations, balancing the visually heavier portions, and letting subtle features add a "now you see them, now you don't" quality.

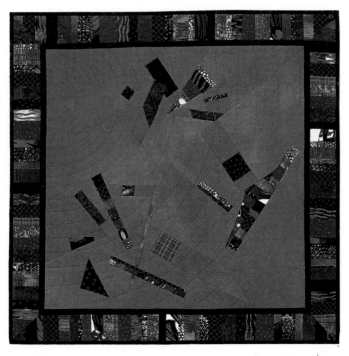

■ *The Sound of Louis Armstrong* by Ursula Reikes, 1997, Issaquah, Washington, 30½" x 30½". Playful, brightly colored pieces float in perfect balance on this dark purple, mottled background. Ursula repeated the bright fabrics in her border, which she structured in a contrasting pattern.

Designing with a Single Shape

There is nothing new or earth-shattering about designing with a single shape. There are many traditional "one-patch" quilts, such as Postage Stamp, Picket Fence, and Grandmother's Flower Garden. But when Grandmother cut the hexagons for her Flower Garden, most likely she cut with the finished quilt in mind: a certain number of yellow hexagons for the flower centers; six times that many prints—in groups of six—to ring the yellow centers. She needed twelve times as many solid-color hexagons in groups of twelve that coordinated with the printed groups of six, and so on. The premise for including a single-shape approach in a design book is to encourage a spontaneous design process—on the wall with precut shapes.

A painter, before stepping up to her easel, squeezes dabs of several colors onto the palette. She doesn't know how much of each color she'll use, or even if she'll use them all, but they're available in case she needs them. She'll replenish some colors many times; others she may never touch.

Precutting fabric of many colors and values in a single shape allows quilters the same spontaneity. So that I don't flagrantly waste my treasured fabric, I cut only six to eight pieces of each before I begin to design. This gives me enough choices for spontaneous experimentation. This way, I don't have to commit all of my one-half-yard piece of out-of-print, egg-yolk-yellow polka dot to 3" equilateral triangles. When you work, keep the rest of your uncut fabric nearby so you can cut more pieces if needed.

Choosing Fabric

Before you choose your fabric, review "Color" on pages 6–9, "Value" on pages 10–11, and "Scale" on pages 12–13. Select a palette that includes a wide range of values. A variety of darks, mediums, and lights allows you to create a composition your eye can track. Remember that value defines a composition.

Choosing a Shape and Size

Squares, rectangles, half-square triangles, and equilateral triangles are among the easiest shapes to cut. The only requirement is that the same shape will fit together to cover the entire surface of a quilt. Hexagons, half-hexagons, parallelograms, some trapezoids, and even some curved shapes, like those in the old Axe Head block, are single shapes that fit together. It's reasonable to trim shapes that fall at the edges of the quilt to square up the sides.

In "Design Principles" on pages 5–19, I urge you to use large, medium, and small spaces in your quilts to vary scale. It may seem contrary to this principle to design with a constant size throughout, but it is possible to join pieces of the same fabric or pieces that are comparable in color and value. Your eye will automatically combine these similar fabrics and see them as one large area.

The shape of the single unit determines the larger design shapes you can create. You can make a large square by combining small squares, rectangles, or half-square triangles. You can't make a square by combining equilateral triangles.

Let's look at the characteristics of a few basic shapes.

Squares

The square is the pre-eminent, quintessential shape in the vocabulary of quilts. It is also among the easiest shapes to cut. I can't imagine a quilter who has not used a square.

You can use the square in a way that emphasizes its nature (as in a black-and-white checkerboard) or in a way that obliterates its nature (as in a watercolor quilt). In the watercolor technique, the outline of each square is disguised because one printed fabric blends into another.

Watercolor fabric squares and black and white checkerboard squares.

The size of the squares you use is part personal preference and part dependent on the projected size of the finished quilt. If you are aiming for a small wall quilt—say 24" x 24" or smaller—you would do better to use a 1½"- to 2"-finished square. If you used a square 3" or larger in a small quilt, you would be limited to designing with just a few pieces. You wouldn't be able to make many transitions or changes. In short, there wouldn't be enough space in which to design. Big quilts can accommodate big squares; for small quilts, stick to small squares.

The obvious limitation of the square is that it isn't possible to use diagonal lines in your design unless you place all your squares on point. OK, maybe "isn't possible" is a challenge to creative quilters. Certainly, you can include diagonal lines, even curved ones, with striped fabric and other prints. You can use prints to add design lines no matter what shape you cut, but prints are perhaps most useful with squares.

You can use prints to provide curved or diagonal lines.

Read the following list of exercises, then brainstorm additional ideas. Try out the ones that interest you most.

- Starting in the center of the design wall, lay out a vertical row of squares of the same fabric. Cross the row at the center with a horizontal row, using the same fabric. Now design the four empty quarters, making each quarter the same for a symmetrical quilt. Border the design with more squares of the fabric you used in the original vertical and horizontal rows.
- Place dark squares at the edges and gradate to light squares in the middle to create the illusion of glowing light behind the center of the quilt. Or create two concentrations of light and/or color.
- Using fabrics printed with curving lines, connect print squares so the curved lines create one or more curved shapes in the quilt.
- Place squares on point on the design wall and build strong diagonal lines in your composition.
- Offset vertical or horizontal rows so they resemble stacks of bricks.
- Make a background of pieced squares, then appliqué or embellish it. Cut squares from strip-pieced units, or cut squares from fabric printed with smaller shapes.

CHAIN PIECING SQUARES

Individually cut and placed squares can seem daunting when it's time to sew them together. Most of us have followed chain-piecing instructions; however, the instructions seldom include moving the pieces from the wall to the machine and back to the wall in the right order. A student taught me this method years ago, and it is the best one I know.

1. Make sure you have only one layer of pieces on your design wall. If you tried out more than one square in a position and left two or more pieces stacked, remove all but your final choices.

2. Place the top square in the second row (the row to the right of the farthest-left row, over the square to its left (the top square in the farthest-left row), right sides together. Think of the two squares as pages in a little book, and "close the book." If your fabric won't stick, pin the squares together.

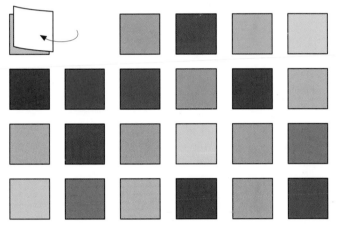

3. Drop down one square and place the square now at the top of vertical row #2 face down over the square to its left, closing the book.

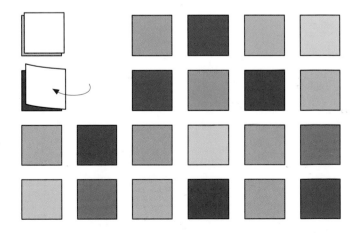

4. Continue closing books in these two vertical rows until the entire second vertical row is face down over the first.

5. Stack the book at the top of the row on the book below it, stack those two books on the book below them, continuing down the row until the squares are stacked in one pile.

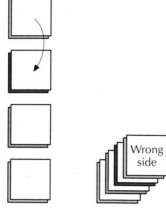

Wrong side

6. Carefully transfer this stack to your sewing machine. Do not turn the stack or lose track of its upper edge. Pick up the top two squares and sew them together along the right edge, using a ¼"-wide seam allowance. Stop at the end of the seam, leaving the fabric under the presser foot. If you can, set your machine to end in the "needle down" position. Do not lift the presser foot or cut the threads. Pick up the next two squares in the stack and place them under the presser foot, with the upper edge butted against, but not overlapping, the previously sewn pair. Continue the line of stitching along the right edge of the second pair of squares.

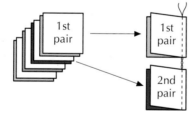

1st pair → 1st pair

2nd pair

7. Continue feeding pairs under your presser foot, one after the next, until you've chained all the pairs together. Remove the chain from the sewing machine. Do not cut the threads between squares.

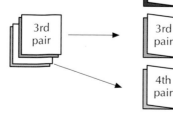

1st pair

2nd pair

3rd pair → 3rd pair

4th pair

8. The only way you can get the squares out of order now is to confuse the top of the chain with the bottom. To prevent this, mark the upper left square with a pin, fabric marker, or sticker—or just memorize the piece of fabric.

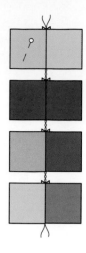

9. Pick up the squares in the next (third) vertical row—now the farthest-left row on your wall—placing the top square, right side up, over the one below it. Place these two squares on top of the one below, right side up, continuing until you have picked up the whole row. Take it to your machine without dropping or turning it.

3rd row

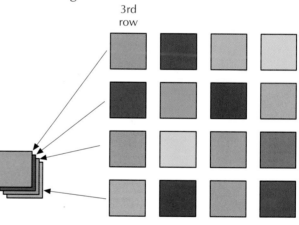

10. Open the top book of the chained squares you pieced in steps 6 and 7. Place the top square of the new stack on top of the opened book's right square ("page"), right sides together. Stitch along the right edge, using a ¼"-wide seam allowance. Continue until you've added the entire stack of squares in the third vertical row.

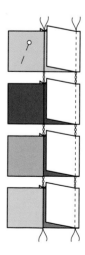

11. Stack the squares in the next (fourth) vertical row and add them to the existing chained rows, the way you did in step 10. Repeat steps 9 and 10 until all the squares are sewn into horizontal rows, connected by threads from the rows above them.

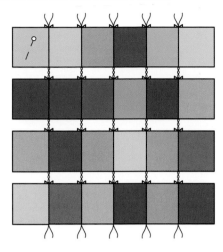

12. Press the seam allowances in each row in opposite directions. The easiest way to do this is to position just the first row at the edge of the ironing board, letting every row below it hang off the edge. Press the seam allowances. Move the chained squares up so row 3 is at the edge of the ironing board. Press rows 1, 3, 5, 7, and 9—continuing until all the odd-numbered rows are pressed in one direction.

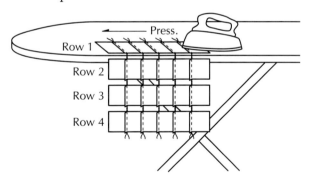

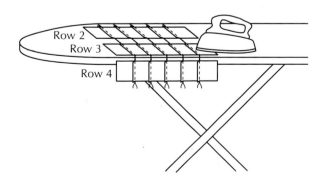

13. Rotate the chained squares and place the first un-pressed row on the edge of the ironing board. Press rows 2, 4, 6, and 8—continuing until all the even-numbered rows are pressed. By rotating the chained unit, you press the seams in the even-numbered rows in the opposite direction from the odd-numbered rows, but your pressing motion remains in the same direction.

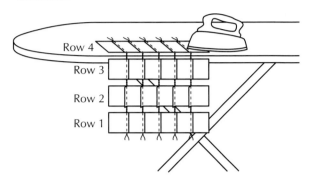

14. Fold row 1 over row 2, right sides together, then pin the two rows together, matching seam intersections. Sew the long horizontal seam. You'll never need to clip the threads holding the rows together, unless you want to press the horizontal seams open.

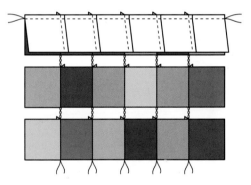

15. Repeat step 14 until you've sewn all the rows together.

Half-Square Triangles

Probably the second most commonly used shape in quiltmaking is the half-square triangle (or isosceles right triangle). To cut this shape, start with a square, then cut it in half once diagonally to make two half-square triangles. If you want your finished triangle to be a specific measurement on its legs (the two short sides), cut the square ⅞" larger on each side than the desired finished measurement, then cut it from corner to corner. When piecing the resulting triangles, use a ¼"-wide seam allowance.

For single-shape projects, I usually choose a round number for the cut size of the square, then cut the squares into triangles. Since all the triangles will fit together when cut identically, it doesn't matter what size the finished square is. Just make sure the size of the finished triangle is appropriate for the projected size of the finished quilt.

The half-square triangle is perhaps the most versatile of quiltmaking shapes. Two of them, cut from the same fabric and joined (or two fabrics similar in color and value) can look like a square, a parallelogram, or a triangle.

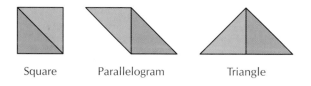

Square Parallelogram Triangle

Combine multiple half-square triangles to make a variety of shapes, determined by the number and arrangement of the triangles.

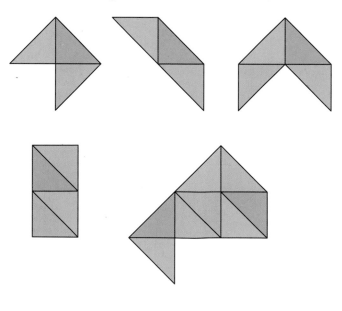

You can combine vertical and horizontal lines with diagonal lines when you use half-square triangles as your single shape.

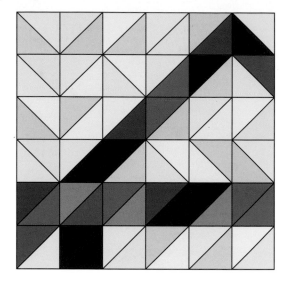

Different prints can give similar designs an entirely different feel. Imagine "Earth" on page 54 with the same value placement but done in floral chintz or Japanese indigo-and-white Yukata cloth.

Take a stack of precut half-square triangles to your design wall and see what you can do with them. Changing the direction of the diagonal seam in each square gives your quilt more interesting movement than a design in which every diagonal seam runs in the same direction. When you have a design that pleases you, record the arrangement to help you replace the pieces correctly after sewing pairs of triangles into squares. A useful method is to draw the direction of the seams in each square, one row at a time. Then add symbols for each of the fabrics used on each side of the lines. Or, take a Polaroid snapshot of

your arrangement, provided you can read the details of individual fabrics well enough to identify them later.

PIECING HALF-SQUARE TRIANGLES

1. I usually record the arrangement of two or three rows at a time, then sew them together. To sew the rows, place the two upper-left triangles right sides together. Repeat for the next two triangles to the right, and continue until all the triangles in the row are paired.

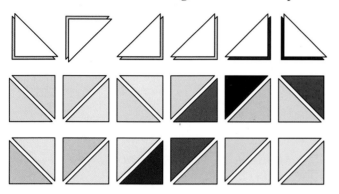

2. Stack the first pair of triangles (at farthest left) on top of the next pair; place the two pairs on top of the third pair, continuing until you've stacked the whole row. At the machine, sew the long edges of the first triangle pair together, chain piece the next pair, and continue until the entire stack is chain pieced. (Refer to steps 6–7 of "Squares" on page 46.)

3. Press the seam allowances open or toward the darker fabric while the squares are still chained together, or cut the chain apart, keeping the squares in order as you press. Replace the pieces on the design wall according to your recorded arrangement and proceed to the next row down.

If the half-square triangles are uneven, trim them to make perfect squares. The squares may come out a little smaller than the intended size, but since you'll cut them identically, it won't matter. Just make sure the seam lies exactly at the square's corners.

To trim half-square triangles, align the diagonal line of a square ruler—such as the Bias Square ruler—with the seam before you cut. Trim two sides, then rotate the square and trim the remaining two sides. Carefully trimmed squares are easy to match at the seams and make a flat quilt.

When you've sewn all of the triangles into squares and replaced them on the wall, chain piece them, referring to steps 2–15 on pages 45–47.

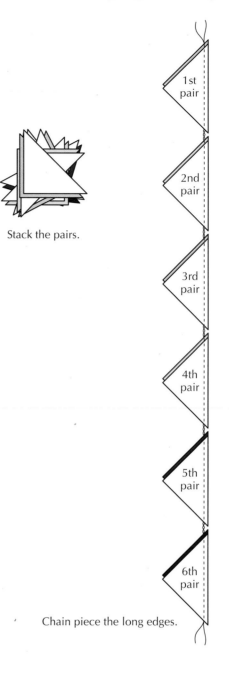

Stack the pairs.

Chain piece the long edges.

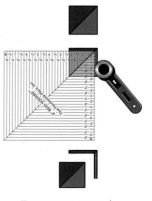

Turn segments and trim opposite two sides.

Equilateral Triangles

What do you remember about equilateral triangles from high school geometry? Well, an equilateral triangle has three equal sides. It also has three equal angles—each 60°. Knowing this helps when it comes to cutting.

CUTTING EQUILATERAL TRIANGLES

1. Cut a straight-of-grain strip of any width. Let's use a 3"-wide strip as an example.

2. Align the 60°-angle mark on your ruler with the edge of the strip, and make the cut.

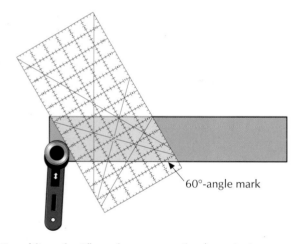

60°-angle mark

3. Align the 3" mark on your ruler (match the measurement to the cut width of your strip) with the 60°-angle cut you just made, and make another cut parallel to the first. You should have a diamond with two 60° angles and two 120° angles.

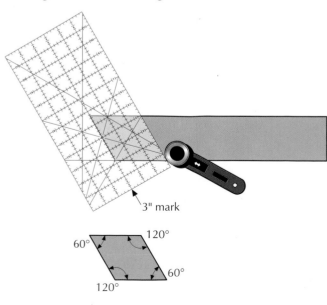

3" mark

120°
60°
60°
120°

4. Cut as many diamonds from different fabrics as you need, then divide each diamond into two equilateral triangles by cutting from point to point across the width of the diamond.

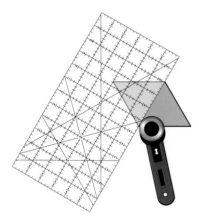

DESIGNING WITH EQUILATERAL TRIANGLES

Placing shapes next to each other that are similar in color, value, and scale allows you to "moosh" fabrics, to gradually change value or color the way you do when making colourwash or watercolor quilts. Combining more than one equilateral triangle of the same, or nearly the same, fabric and placing these against a contrasting background allows you to create a variety of shapes. Here are a few possibilities:

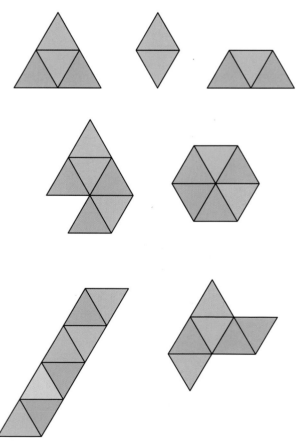

Like any other single shape, equilateral triangles can be used to design symmetrical or asymmetrical quilts. Build your design by placing one side of the equilateral triangles parallel to the top and bottom edges of the quilt, or parallel to the sides of the quilt. The way you place the triangles on the design wall will determine whether you sew vertical, horizontal, or diagonal rows when you assemble your quilt. When assembling the quilt, remember to look for straight seams rather than colors that go together visually, or you may need to sew set-in seams.

Use the equilateral triangle when you want something gentler than blunt 90° or sharp 45° angles. When using a 60° angle, it's natural for the eye to keep turning back to the inside of the composition, completing revolutions, connecting focal points. Already I can hear those wheels turning in your heads as you try to upset that logic. Perhaps you are dreaming up compositions of equilateral triangles that create high drama with restless images. Send me pictures!

Seeing Connections and Sewing Connections

Our eyes and our brains connect like things. In this small design made of equilateral triangles, similar or identical fabrics connect visually to form diamonds, parallelograms, trapezoids, and other complex shapes.

The impulse to connect the similar-fabric triangles is so strong that beginning quiltmakers often want to sew them together first when constructing the section.

Of course, this creates the need to do set-in seams. Avoid set-in seams by separating the section into horizontal rows; then you'll have to sew only straight lines.

Rectangles

Rectangles provide the greatest challenge when used as a single-shape design unit. When we add the ¼"-wide seam allowance to all four sides, the proportions of the rectangle change. You need to allow for the seam allowances when designing on the wall. I recommend designing with a rectangle that is a modular size, for example, one in which four finished widths equal one finished length. This way, you can sew four of them together, side by side, to make a square.

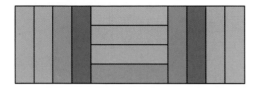

When you place these rectangles on your design wall, raw edge to raw edge in groups of four, they aren't modular. This is because their seam allowances add extra width and length. Placed with raw edges together, four combined widths are much longer than one length. If you group four rectangles side by side and arrange them so their long edges are perpendicular to the long edges of an adjacent group of four rectangles, the grouping won't be modular.

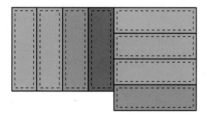

Any arrangement of rectangles on your design wall will be misleading if you align them raw edge to raw edge, so always overlap rectangles by a seam allowance as you design. More importantly, adopt the attitude that you are open to surprises; it's less frustrating when you must do some compensatory designing and sewing.

Below are a few suggestions for arranging rectangles and considering the placement of seam lines. In all of these illustrations, the lines indicate seams, not raw edges.

Another way to use rectangles is to sew groups of four modular rectangles into squares before you approach the design wall. You can use similar, alternating, gradated, or mixed values; all brights, all neutrals, or any other fabric combination. Then design with the pieced squares.

Rectangles can be a challenge, but then doesn't some of our best work happen in response to a challenge?

Additional Design Ideas

If, after you've designed your single-shape quilt on the wall, you feel it needs a shape smaller than the basic unit, here are a few options:

- Divide your basic shape into smaller parts in a few places.
- Appliqué a few smaller, floating shapes on top of your pieced shapes.
- Find a fabric printed to look like it's divided into smaller shapes and use it in your quilt.
- Strip piece fabrics together, then cut the single shape from the pieced unit.

In my experience, designing with a single shape is one of those exercises that often cries out for deviation. I never consider the border to be part of the single-shape exercise, and on many occasions, I've felt the need to divide a single shape into two or more smaller shapes. Detouring from the exercise long enough to appliqué winding tendrils of bias tape over your single-shape quilt is to acknowledge that there are no Quilt Police. Nor is there any all-powerful Queen Quilt Teacher who will banish you from the fabric store or quilt guild if you break the sacred commandments of the Exercise. Experiment and enjoy!

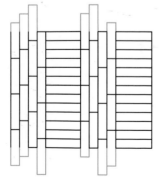
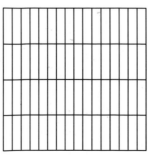
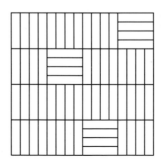
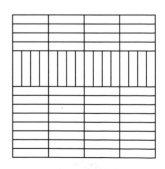

■ *Red Window* by Sharon Pelton, 1989, Seattle, Washington, 39" x 57". This entire quilt—except for the black inner strip—is made of half-square triangles placed so that the hypotenuse is vertical. The illusion of transparency in the red rectangle makes the gorgeous asymmetrical composition even more stunning. (Collection of Harold A. Pelton.)

■ *Looking Southwest* by Lynell Arnott, 1997, Bellevue, Washington, 33" x 41". Lynell used a modular rectangle—four finished widths equal one finished length. Changing values vary the rail-fence arrangement.

■ *Kanji* by Lorraine Torrence, 1988, Seattle, Washington, 45" x 38". I mixed vintage kimono fabrics with domestic cottons. Two triangles near the center are subdivided to provide a few small spaces. Lines extend to the edges, keeping the border an integral part of the piece.

■ Untitled quilt by Jennifer Younger, 1997, Seattle, Washington, 32" x 32". Single-shape compositions designed spontaneously on the wall don't have to be asymmetrical. This beautifully colored piece has just enough value variation and unpredictable changes in fabric to keep us on our toes.

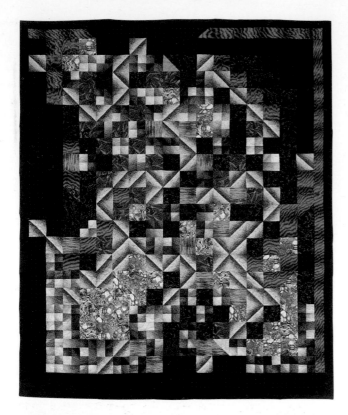

■ *Crossing Paths* by Debbie Hodin, 1997, Spokane, Washington, 60" x 72". Debbie achieves strong movement with diagonal prints. With the exception of the three four-patch squares, all the pieces are the same size. Even the neutral-colored squares that look like four small pieces are one printed fabric.

■ *Earth* by Reynola Pakusich, 1997, Bellingham, Washington, 42" x 55½". Rusty red triangles at the lower left and upper right subtly accent more neutral colors. The varied stripe adds a clever change of scale.

■ *Reflections* by Lorraine Torrence, 1997, Seattle, Washington, 40½" x 40½"; machine quilted by Gretchen Engle. I arranged the rectangles in this piece horizontally, except for the horizontal row of vertical rectangles just above the center line. Smaller border rectangles and appliquéd black squares vary the scale.

■ *Mostly Mountains* by Manya Powell, 1997, Spokane, Washington, 43" x 38". In this piece, diagonal seams create movement. All seventy-two squares have diagonal seams, but only eleven are oriented differently from the rest. Those important diagonals are made more noticeable through high-contrast divisions. Without these eleven seams, the piece would not move. Without the addition of light in the dark lower-left corner, or dark in the light upper-right corner, the two areas would not be having a conversation.

■ *Equilateral Escapades* by Cheryl Poffenroth, 1997, Spokane, Washington, 36" x 30". Combining lots of light fabrics enabled Cheryl to create big, medium, and small spaces. The varied scale of the prints makes interesting texture in her summery, gardenlike scene.

■ *Cranes and Mountains* by Karen Pederson, 1992, Seattle, Washington, 35" x 46". The interior breaks through to the border in this beautiful asymmetrical composition. The Japanese word *shibui* seems appropriate for this piece—elegant simplicity.

■ Untitled triptych by Ronda Newitt-Larson, 1997, Everett, Washington, 47" x 40½". The wonderful asymmetrical composition is matched by great use of color. A dusty pink triangle in the upper middle panel is an inspired repetition of the red piece below it (in a different value), providing unexpected depth in the midst of neutral ochers.

■ *Reverberation* by Lorraine Torrence, 1997, Seattle, Washington, 37" x 26¾". Squares cut from fabric printed with straight or curving lines direct the eye in this piece. Color links the two design areas: the black-and-white area contains a little red and yellow, and the red-and-yellow area contains a little black and white.

Multi-View Images

The Multi-View Lens was introduced to quilters in the late 1980s. A transparent piece of plastic about the size of letter paper, it is divided into twenty-five squares, arranged in a 5 x 5 layout, and has a large magnifying rectangle at the bottom. When viewed through the lens, an image is multiplied twenty-five times.

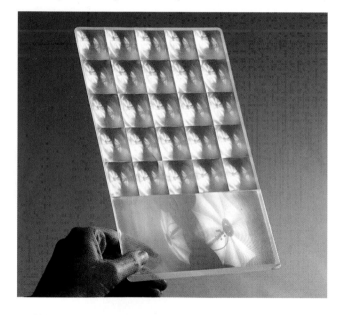

The quilt world uses the Multi-View Lens to see how a unit will look in a repetitive-block quilt. The fallacy of this, however, is that the image one sees in the upper-left square of the lens is not the same as the image in the lower-right square. The image shifts so that different parts of it are visible in different squares. The pattern is a repetitive but changing image.

When I first looked through a Multi-View Lens, it occurred to me that I could use it in three ways: to see the world abstractly—as shapes, repetitions, colors, and values; to gather repetitive patterns; and to see how a single image would look as a group of shifting patterns.

Few of us see the world abstractly. When we see an object, we impose on it what we know about it. This often prevents our seeing things the way they really are. How often have you looked through your camera's viewfinder at a quilt hanging on the garage door, only to find later when your pictures are developed that there was a shadow covering one corner of the quilt? You didn't notice the shadow when you looked through the camera viewfinder, but it was there.

We see selectively. We fill in the blanks. We visually complete unfinished things. We need to learn to see.

To make a Multi-View Image quilt, I repeat a simplified design in each of nine 15" squares, trimming each square differently to make 12" x 12" blocks. The resulting quilt mimics the shifting images seen through a Multi-View Lens.

Assembling Tools and Materials

In addition to your design wall, sewing machine, and iron and ironing board, you need the following supplies to make a Multi-View Image quilt:

- Multi-View Lens
- Sketchbook and pencil
- 15" x 15" piece of paper (brown craft paper or newsprint work well)
- Rotary cutter, cutting mat, 24"-long rotary ruler
- A selection of fabrics varied in value, color, and scale; cuts of ½ yd. or larger are best
- ½"-wide drafting or artist's tape
- Permanent black marking pen
- The great outdoors, the great indoors, or magazine pictures

Exceedingly convenient but optional:
- 15"-square ruler
- Plastic template material
- Polaroid camera

Using the Multi-View Lens

Looking through a Multi-View Lens, you are more apt to see an abstract pattern (repeated images of shapes, colors, lines, and spaces) than to identify the subject matter. We seldom look through a Multi-View Lens and really see details of tables, people, or trees—whatever objects are there. The pattern predominates and allows us to see the design elements. We see the subject abstractly.

As you look around you through the Multi-View Lens, rotate it one way, then the other, so you see the multiplied image straight and tipped diagonally in both directions. Find the compositions and orientations that most please you. My preference is usually for designs that emphasize diagonals; I find them more dynamic. Using diagonals is also an easy way to avoid vertical and horizontal elements that link from block to block and extend across the entire quilt, which can be difficult to align.

Shown below are some familiar objects, and the same objects seen through a Multi-View Lens.

After you discover a repetitive design you like, sketch the image visible in one of the squares of the Multi-View Lens. This doesn't require the ability to draw well; just try to approximate the major lines and shapes. Now put down the lens and draw the image again, cleaning it up for use as a quilt block. Use the first sketch—not the image seen through the lens—as your design source. Simplify the design by eliminating details that would be difficult to piece.

Draw the design again, this time on a 15" square of paper. Try to use round, easy-to-find-on-a-ruler measurements. Trace the final lines of the design with a permanent black marking pen. This is your master drawing.

Simplify your piecing task by extending at least one of the design lines across the block, from one edge to another. Mentally separate the block at this line to see if each remaining section has at least one line that goes all the way across it. Continue dividing the design into sections, looking for lines that go all the way across.

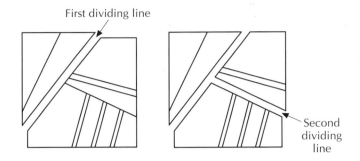

First dividing line

Second dividing line

If you can't find a seam line that goes from edge to edge in a section, you might want to add one. Find a place where the fabric on both sides of this new seam will be the same. This way, you'll avoid having to set in seams. If you need to add any seams, draw a dotted line on your master drawing to indicate the added seam.

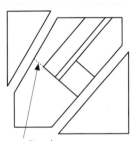

Add a seam line here.

FAMILIAR OBJECTS, AND THE SAME OBJECTS SEEN THROUGH A MULTI-VIEW LENS.

Setting in Pieces

If adding a seam to make the piecing easier compromises your design, go ahead and set in the piece. Mark the pivot point on the wrong side of each fabric. Clip to the pivot point on the inside angle as shown. With right sides together, align pivot points. Stitch to the pivot point, stop with the needle in the fabric, then lift the presser foot. Pivot the fabric and stitch the remaining seam.

sary, then place the needle in the other side of the seam at the pivot point. Take a few stitches, backstitch, then continue stitching the remaining seam.

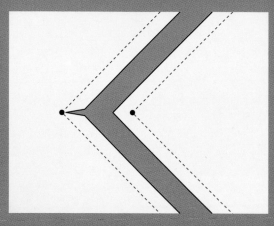

Mark pivot points on wrong side of fabric.

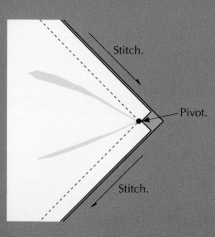

Stitch.

Pivot.

Stitch.

If there is a seam where you are setting in a piece, leave the seam allowance open from the pivot point to the edges of the fabric instead of clipping. Stitch to the pivot point, backstitch, then remove the fabric from the machine. Adjust the pieces if neces-

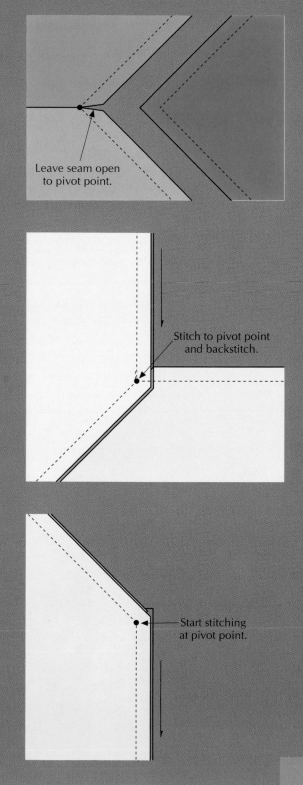

Leave seam open to pivot point.

Stitch to pivot point and backstitch.

Start stitching at pivot point.

Choosing Fabrics

The design source often suggests fabrics for your block, especially if your design is fairly representational (mottled or hand-dyed blue for sky, leafy-green print for trees). This is a perfectly fine way to choose fabric, as long as you can abandon the original image if the piece needs an odd color to spruce it up or an unusual fabric to provide scale variety. Remember, the original image you saw through the lens was just a starting place, not a picture to be rendered perfectly.

For Multi-View Image quilts to be most successful, there should be some contrast in two opposite corners: dark and light, bright and dull, or patterned and plain. A contrast in value is the most dramatic and will provide the most movement when you trim the blocks.

Select a group of fabrics and do the Fold-and-View test: Place folded or wadded fabrics in their intended locations, right on the master drawing, to get an idea of what they'll look like together.

Another way to make tentative color and fabric choices is to photocopy the master drawing, reducing it to fit on letter-size paper. Using colored pencils, fill in the design with different colors and values. Later, you can paste fabric pieces that have been cut to fit the spaces on the drawing. Make nine mock-ups of your favorite block to see how it will work in a quilt. You can even fold your paper blocks to see how they'll look when trimmed, following the diagram on page 62.

When you've selected your fabrics for each location in the block, note your choices on the master drawing.

Cutting Fabrics

If you have a limited amount of fabric, making a template for each design segment is the most economical way to work. Place plastic template material over the master drawing and trace each piece, leaving at least ½" between pieces for seam allowances. On the template, make notes to help you (right side, fabric choice, number to cut, directional fabric lines). Add ¼"-wide seam allowances around each template, unless you wish to draw seam lines and eyeball the seam allowance when you cut the fabric.

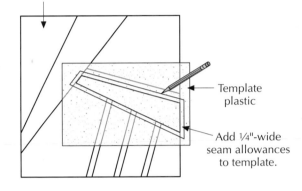

Master drawing

Template plastic

Add ¼"-wide seam allowances to template.

FOLDED FABRICS

AFTER TRYING OUT A FEW COLORATIONS, I DECIDED TO ELIMINATE ALL COLOR FROM ONE CORNER.

Strip Piecing Sections

Using your 15" x 15" master drawing, identify an area of the design you could make as a pieced unit. This usually means a section with one seam and two fabrics or a section with more than one parallel seam and more than two fabrics. You can strip piece these sections, then cut the combination unit from the strip set.

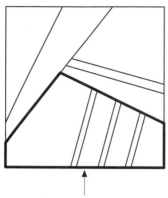

Strip piece this section.

Measure the width of the finished strips (perpendicular to the seam lines) on your master drawing.

Cut strips from your selected fabrics, adding ¼ " to each edge for seam allowances. Add a generous ½ " to the width of the strip set's first and last strips.

Sew the strips together to make strip sets. It often takes more than one strip set of the same fabric combination to yield nine identical sections.

Make a see-through template of the section from the master drawing. Mark the section's seam lines on the template. Place the template on the strip set, aligning the marks with the strip set's seam lines. Use this template to cut identical pieces for each block.

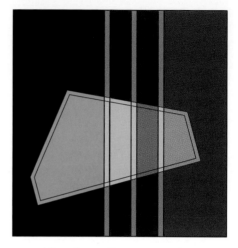

Align drawn lines on template with seam lines in strip set.

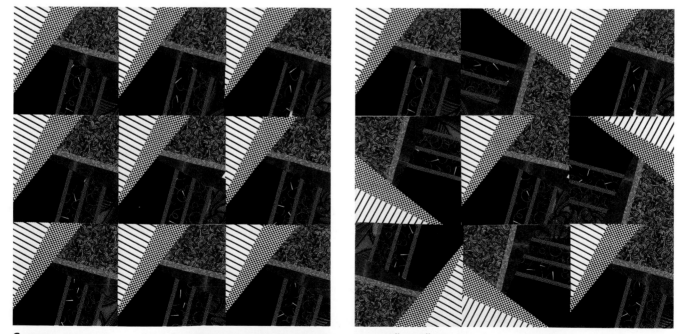

CONSIDER YOUR BLOCKS IN DIFFERENT ARRANGEMENTS BEFORE TRIMMING THEM TO 12" X 12" BLOCKS.

Assembling and Cutting the Blocks

After completing all the sections for each of the blocks, assemble the blocks. When trimming the blocks to 15" squares, you must trim each identically. Place a 15" square ruler on the master drawing. On the ruler, align pieces of tape with a few of the block's seams for reference.

Place the 15"-square ruler on top of the squares, one at a time, aligning the tape on the ruler with the reference seams on the squares. It may help to draw arrows on the tape indicating which side aligns with the seam line. Trim the edges of all the squares to make identical 15" x 15"

blocks (don't worry about small irregularities).

Put the blocks on your design wall edge to edge, all oriented in the same direction. Record the arrangement with a Polaroid snapshot, or simply make a mental note of how successful the design is as a group. Rearrange and consider the blocks in different configurations.

When you decide on a set, experiment with the blocks in the shifting-image arrangement suggested by the Multi-View Lens. Fold under the edges along the suggested trimming lines as shown in the diagram on page 62.

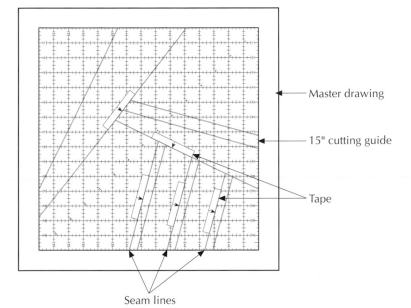

Master drawing

15" cutting guide

Tape

Seam lines

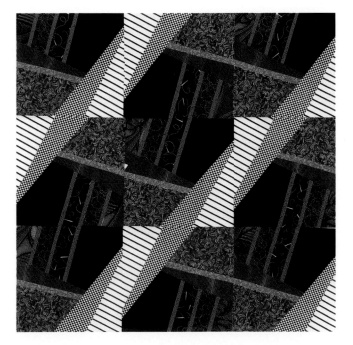 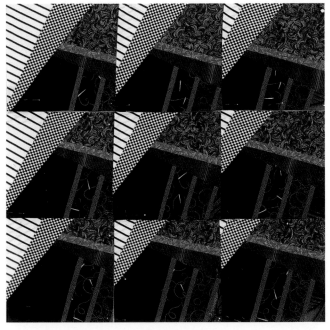

If you like the shifted image arrangements, trim the blocks following the diagram at right. Pin or tape a number to the center of each block to indicate its placement.

Trim the blocks according to the diagram, or design your own trimming pattern. Trim each block to measure exactly 12" x 12". Cut off the widest edge of each block first, to make the best use of the trimmings later. After you trim the blocks, replace them in position on the design wall.

If the nine blocks look great placed edge to edge, sew them together. Occasionally, the blocks are complicated or "busy" enough that sashing is needed to separate and calm them down. (See "Volcano" by Gretchen Engle on page 66.)

Borders

With the quilt on your design wall, try out border options. The block trimmings are usually good elements to use in the borders since they are related to the body of the quilt. Including them can balance or emphasize the blocks.

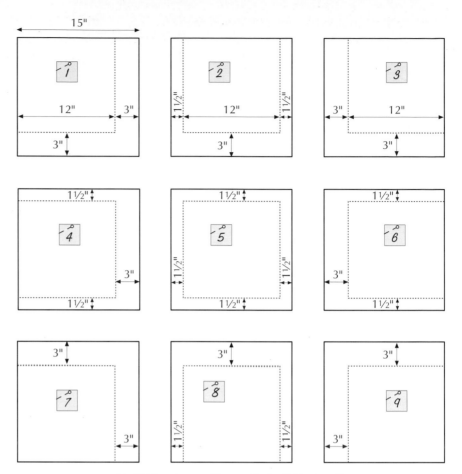

Multi-View Lens cutting guide for 9-block quilt
(15" x 15" original block, cut to 12" x 12")

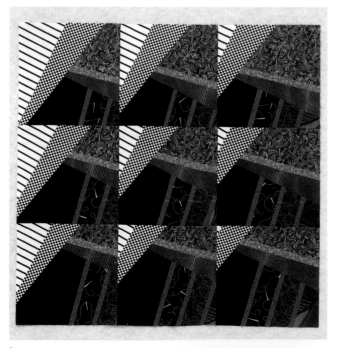

If the blocks look great placed edge to edge, sew together.

Audition border ideas on your design wall.

It's common to want to use the trimmings exactly as they came off the blocks. But by trimming them further, you might create more interesting effects and increase the impact of your quilt. For example, you can cut out all the dark sections and sew them together, providing an enlarged dark area to wrap around a light corner of the quilt or to augment a dark corner.

You might alternate little pieces of small-scale, colorful trimmings with one of the fabrics. Placing this combination near a plain edge will create a variation of scale.

Sometimes I group all the trimmings of one color or value opposite the concentration of that color in the quilt to balance the design. On other occasions, I place trimmings of one color or value in the corner where that color or value shows in the blocks. Doing this emphasizes a color or value in a certain location, and you can create balance in other ways. In any case, audition all your design ideas for the border on your design wall and make those visual decisions visually!

Design Pointers

■ After you draw your design on the 15" square of paper, roll the paper so that the top and bottom edges come together. You'll see how the lines at the edges will relate to each other when the blocks are placed side by side. Do lines meet at the edges, creating uninterrupted horizontal (or vertical) lines? Would the lines extend across the quilt?

■ Designs with predominating diagonal lines are usually most interesting.

■ If you choose to trim the blocks, highly contrasting opposite corners generally increase the illusion that the blocks shift across the quilt. Contrast can be in value, color, intensity, texture—whatever changes in predominance as the blocks shift.

■ If you place a dominant element in the center of the block, chances are it will stay untrimmed. Therefore, it won't change much from block to block and could be boring. Dominant elements are more effective when placed toward the edges—as you trim the blocks, the dominant element changes size, making the shift more obvious.

■ An element must extend at least 3½" from the edge of the block in order to remain visible in all nine blocks after they are trimmed to 12". Anything closer to the edge than 3" will disappear entirely when a 3"-wide strip is trimmed from some of the blocks.

■ A shift of less than 1½" is usually not noticeable.

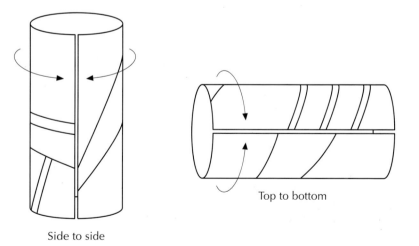

Side to side

Top to bottom

Variations in the Size or Number of Blocks

Making 9 blocks, each 15" x 15", and cutting them into 12" x 12" blocks is certainly not the only option for Multi-View Image quilts. The shifting image can be even more dramatic with 16 blocks, 25 blocks, or even 36 blocks. These alterations require a change in the designing and cutting mathematics. Here's a formula a student handed me as I was explaining how to calculate new numbers for different sizes of original and cut blocks (or rows containing a different number of blocks):

$$\frac{(Y - Z)}{(n - 1)"} = X$$

Y is the size of the original block, Z is the size of the cut block, n is the number of blocks in a row, and X is the amount of shift in inches.

Calm down . . . this isn't so hard! Plug in the numbers of our original exercise and it's clear:

$$\frac{(15" - 12")}{(3 - 1)"} = \frac{3"}{2"} = 1\frac{1}{2}"$$

Each time we trimmed the 12" block from the 15" block, we moved the edges in increments of 1½". Right? Right. Check the cutting diagram on page 62.

If you want to change the scenario, you must know three of the four unknowns. Usually you know at least two of them because they are changes you want to make deliberately. For instance, you may want a total of 16 blocks instead of 9: 4 blocks by 4 blocks. So the quantity "n" is now 4. Perhaps you also know that you want to maintain a 1½" shift. There's the "X" quantity. And keeping the cut size of the block at 12" suits you. That means "Z" is 12". All you have to determine is "Y" or the size of the original block. Now our formula reads:

$$\frac{(Y - 12")}{(4 - 1)"} = 1\frac{1}{2}" \quad OR \quad \frac{(Y - 12")}{3"} = 1\frac{1}{2}"$$

To get the total quantity above the line in the equation, multiply the "n - 1" number, in this example 3", by the amount of the shift: 1½" x 3"= 4½". So we know Y - 12 = 4½. Adding 4½" to 12" gives us the original block size, or Y, which is 16½".

If you want to make a rectangular block or a rectangular quilt with a different number of blocks going across and down, you have to work the formula twice—once for horizontal and once for vertical, with the appropriate numbers plugged in each time.

Don't you wish you had paid more attention in high school algebra? If our high school math teachers had had us make quilts as class projects, it might have been more interesting to those who hated math!

Remember the Rockettes

Remember the Radio City Music Hall Rockettes from New York City (see page 18)? I like to remind students that a single dancer kicking up her leg is not so interesting. The gesture is too simple to be exciting. But twenty-five dancers in a row—all doing that same simple gesture? A knockout! Your block doesn't have to be terribly complicated. Simple is great. It's the repetition of that block that's going to make it a knockout. And the fact that each block shifts and changes slightly is all the more compelling.

■ "Matanuska Valley" by Shirley Heintzman, 1997, Wasilla, Alaska, 44" x 44". Subordinate diagonals soften strong verticals and horizontals in these landscape-inspired blocks. Using trimmings in only one corner makes the border interesting.

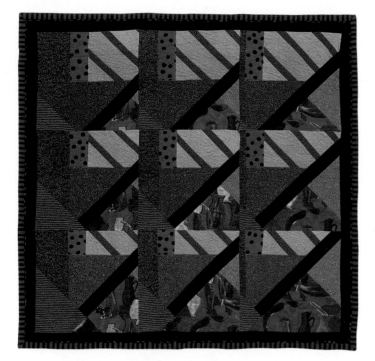

■Untitled Multi-View images by Miriam Kopec, 1994, Renton, Washington, 37" x 37"; machine quilted by Sue Pelton. This is an exceptionally strong design with every directional movement countered by another. The changing values of the orange Pointillist Palette fabric enhance the drama of the trimmed blocks, which didn't need a pieced border to complete the design.

■*Echoes* by Marilyn Hollenback, 1994, Bellevue, Washington, 46" x 46". The large-scale African print lends excitement to an already strong design.

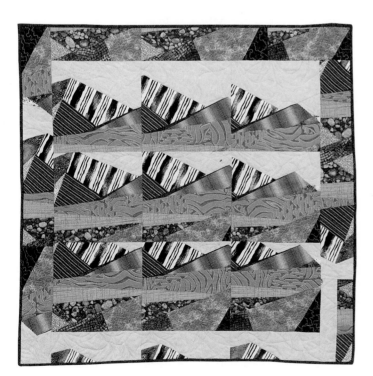

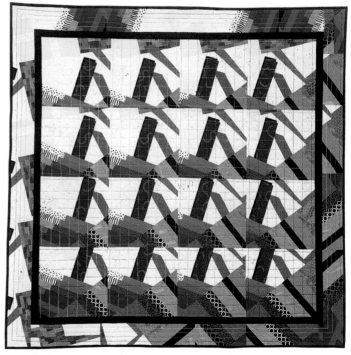

■ *Multi-View Ansel Adams* by Michele Koppelman, 1995, Sharon, Massachusetts, 36" x 36". Michele got her inspiration from a black-and-white Ansel Adams photograph. The varied scale of the printed fabric enhances the design. (Collection of David and Cindi Kaplan)

■ *Multi-View Images: Over and Over* by Lorraine Torrence, 1995, Seattle, Washington, 56" x 56". In this 16-block Multi-View Images quilt, the formula had to change somewhat to allow more room for the shift. Topstitched cordonnet creates a machine-quilted grid as it moves across the quilt, changing from white to black. The white fabric looked too flat at first, so I splattered it with India ink, adding the texture I wanted.

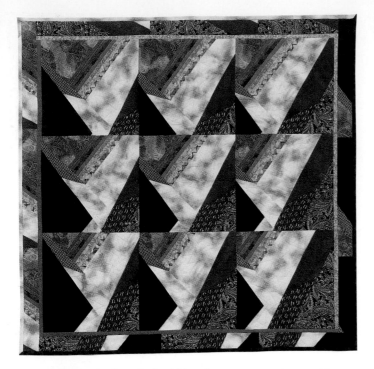

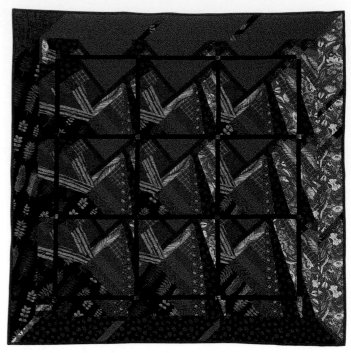

■ *Angles* by Mical Middaugh, 1994, Seattle, Washington, 41" x 41". The black in the right-hand border balances the strong black triangles on the left-hand side of the quilt. The most delicious thing about this quilt is the unexpected pink among the earthy browns and rusts.

■ *Volcano* by Gretchen Engle, 1994, Seattle, Washington, 48" x 48". Dark, narrow strips separate busy blocks and add unity and small spaces to the quilt. Little yellow strips relate the bottom border to the top.

■ *Sharing Secrets* by Linda Ettinger, 1994, Redmond, Washington, 56" x 56½". Linda found her blocks were stronger left untrimmed. The large-scale Japanese print and the small-scale prints make a pleasing combination. Linda repeated the large black-and-white stripe in the center of the quilt with the small one in the border.

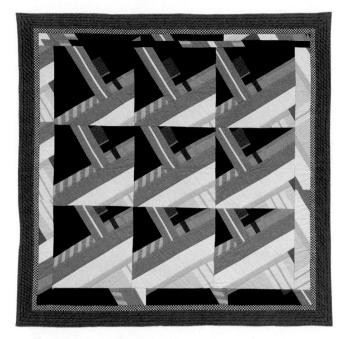

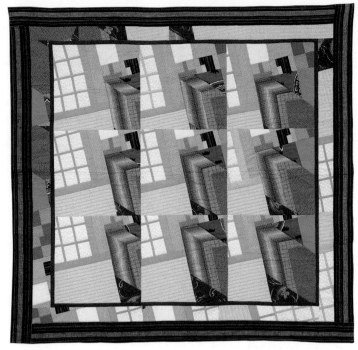

■ *Multi-View Images: Sitka Cabin* by Lorraine Torrence, 1992, Seattle, Washington, 43½" x 43½". This quilt was my first attempt to use the Multi-View Lens as a design tool. While teaching in Alaska, I stayed in an isolated cabin. At night, the cabin's interior was reflected in the windows, providing the inspiration for this piece.

■ *Multi-View Images: Carey* by Lorraine Torrence, 45" x 44". To balance the value, I placed purple trimmings in the border opposite the concentration of purple in the quilt. I did the same with the green trimmings.

■ *Tribal Rhythms* by Christine Davis, 1994, Spokane, Washington, 49" x 42". Instead of trimming them, Christine used two and a half blocks in each row and flipped each one to produce movement. Great color, scale variety, and repetition.

Improving the Checkerboard

The checkerboard pattern has been a staple in designers' tool kits for centuries. The familiar arrangement of squares in alternating values has been used by visual artists in all media: painters, interior decorators, architects, weavers, and fabric printers.

Quilters have made great use of the checkerboard, too, often changing it to spice up the design's predictable nature. Jan Myers-Newbury, for example, has made a career of using the checkerboard theme with superb hand-dyed gradations.

I challenge you to think of the checkerboard—or any pattern—as a springboard. A single idea or just a word can start a brainstorming process. From that process, you can discover so many variations on a theme that you'll be busy the rest of your life.

The Fundamental Checkerboard

Once you activate your checkerboard antennae, you'll find countless versions of printed and woven checkerboards in fabric stores.

Stormy Skies over Black Butte by Jan Myers-Newbury, 1986, Pittsburgh, Pennsylvania, 60" x 36". Using her own hand-dyed gradations, Jan Myers-Newbury has so masterfully explored the checkerboard that I am tempted to say she "owns" it! Illusions of depth and transparency are elegantly executed in her quilts. (Collection of Jim and Barbara Snow; photo by Sam Newbury)

You don't have to depend on prints for your checkerboards; you can make your own. An identical-width striped fabric makes it easy.

Making checkerboards from striped fabric is simpler than making checkerboards from two solid fabrics. Measure the printed stripe to make sure all the stripes are the same width. Add ½" to the width of the printed stripe and cut strips to this measurement, perpendicular to the stripe. Offset the alternating colors and sew the strips together, using a ¼"-wide seam allowance. Pin often to match the corners.

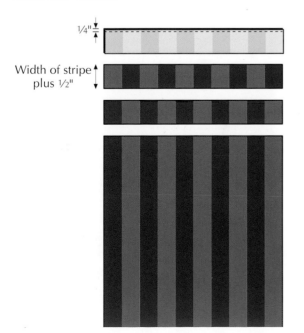

Choosing Fabric for Checkerboards

To make a checkerboard from scratch, first consider fabric. A subtle checkerboard requires fabrics close in value: medium gray and medium tan, royal blue and royal purple, or mossy green and teal green for example. If you want to showcase appliqué, close-value checkerboards are generally better than high-contrast checkerboards, providing a slightly undulating, understated background. High-contrast fabrics make dramatic checkerboards. Keep in mind that two bright colors, like red and hot pink, might not necessarily make a high-contrast checkerboard. Instead, they might make a fine background for appliqué in cool-but-intense blues, greens, and purples.

The main consideration in pairing high-contrast fabrics is value. Black and white, deep purple and yellow, cobalt blue and bright orange are all high-contrast pairs.

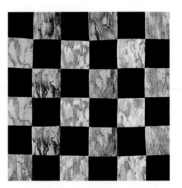

Printed fabrics also make fine checkerboards. Consider scale when you pair printed fabrics. The more the scale varies, the more obvious the checkerboard pattern. Two prints that are similar in scale can provide subtle texture to the checkerboard.

What about making a checkerboard out of only one fabric? We already know cutting a stripe into strips and offsetting the two colors is one way to do it. Here's another way to create alternating squares with stripes or other directional fabrics.

Many fabrics are available that change value from selvage to selvage. Try cutting strips of such a fabric from selvage to selvage, alternating the direction of the value gradation in the strips and sewing them into a strip set. From the strip set, cut segments perpendicular to the seams, then rotate alternating segments before sewing them into a checkerboard.

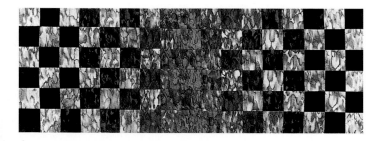

You might be able to use a single fabric for a pieced checkerboard if the right and wrong sides are dramatically different.

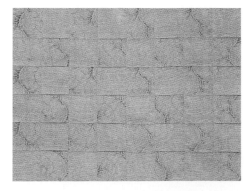

Making Checkerboards

To make a checkerboard, follow these simple steps:

1. Determine the size of your checkerboard's finished square and add ½" to that measurement. Cut an even number of strips of this width from two fabrics. Stacking the fabrics is an efficient way to cut them.

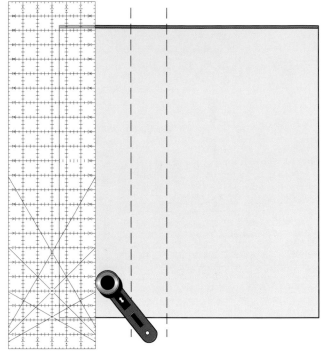

2. Sew alternate fabric strips together, right sides together, using a scant ¼"-wide seam allowance. Press all the seam allowances in one direction.

1/4"

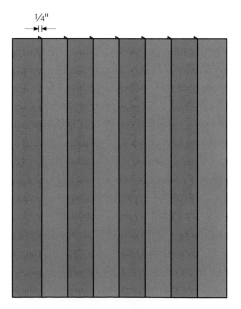

3. From the strip set, cut perpendicular segments the same width as the cut width of the strips.

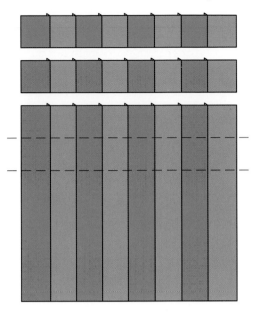

4. Rotate alternating segments so they alternate colors. Sew the segments together, using a ¼"-wide seam allowance. Press seams open or in one direction.

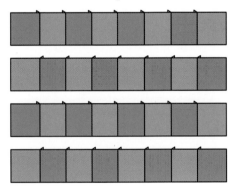

Tip:
"Lock" the opposing seam allowances so the squares match exactly at the seams.

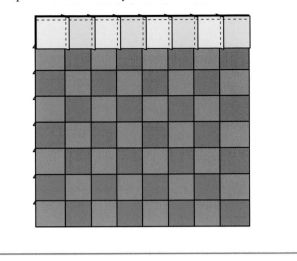

Use your manufactured checkerboard as a design element in a large piece or as a background for other elements. I'm sure you'll think of many other applications and uses!

Design Exercises

Here are some exercises for "Improving the Checkerboard." I've included technical information for the benefit of less-experienced quilters.

■ Add appliqués to a low-contrast checkerboard. Can you think of an effective way to add appliqué to a high-contrast checkerboard and maintain its visibility on the background?

Hint: Hand appliqué would be my choice on a pieced background. Because of all the seam allowances, machine appliqué is troublesome. If machine appliqué is the method you prefer, however, iron a piece of freezer paper to the back of the checkerboard to stabilize it so it will feed more smoothly through the machine.

Try topstitched appliqué, blind-hem-stitch appliqué, or machine blanket-stitch appliqué for best results. I don't recommend satin-stitch appliqué. The stitches may tend to bunch up where they cross the checkerboard's intersecting seam lines.

TOPSTITCH APPLIQUÉ

BLIND-HEM-STITCH APPLIQUÉ

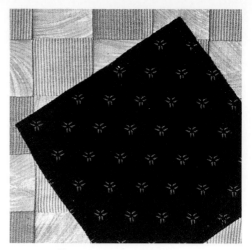

BLANKET-STITCH APPLIQUÉ

■ Paint, draw, stencil, stamp, or stitch on your checkerboard.

Hint: Two very different design elements may not look unified unless you repeat the combination in another way. For example, if you stencil a motif on a pieced checkerboard, consider stenciling the same motif in a different scale on the border.

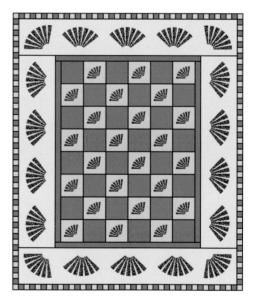

■ Disrupt a checkerboard's static repetition by exchanging some of the squares for others of different colors.

Hint: Complete the first and second steps of making a pieced checkerboard by sewing strips of alternating colors together and cutting perpendicular segments. Rotate the cut rows, but don't sew them together. Put them on your design wall. Place squares of other colors—or even pieced squares—on top of squares in the pieced segments. When you are satisfied with the design, remove the unwanted squares and sew in the new ones. Sew the pieced segments together using ¼"-wide seam allowances.

■ Change the shape of the checkerboard by cutting strips of different widths, for both the strip sets and the perpendicular segments.

Hint: Increase or decrease strip widths in a systematic gradation. Plan the finished sizes of the strips, then add seam allowances to each: ¼" (cut ¾"), ½" (cut 1"), ¾" (cut 1¼"), 1" (cut 1½"), and 1¼" (cut 1¾").

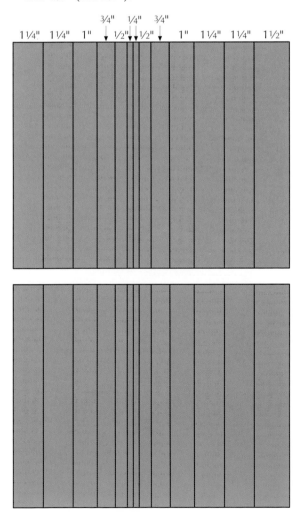

If you have an even number of strips, they are symmetrical across the width of the strip set, and there are two strips of the same width in the middle, rotate the cut sections to make the checkerboard. If the strip set is not symmetrical, you must make two strip sets identical in strip measurements but opposite in color placement.

■ Cut organic shapes from a pieced or printed checkerboard. Fuse or appliqué the shapes on a checkerboard background that is worked in a different scale or color combination.

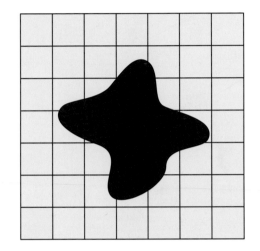

■ Make one or more checkerboards and cut them up. Add other fabrics (or not) and piece them together.

Hint: To experiment with checkerboard designs, take several pictures of a pieced checkerboard, cut them apart, then tape them back together in different arrangements.

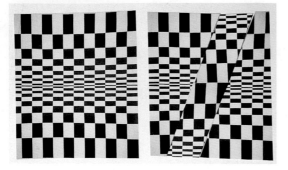

■ Make a checkerboard of different sizes (or colors) of checkerboards.

Note: If you want to make a modular checkerboard, that is, one in which the scale doubles at regular intervals, remember to plan the design based on the finished size of the squares. Then add seam allowances. The ¼"-wide seam allowance stays. A ¾" checkerboard is made from 1¼"-wide strips, a 1½" checkerboard is made from 2"-wide strips, and a 3" checkerboard is made from 3½"-wide strips. The finished sizes of the squares should double in succession: ¾", 1½", 3". The cut sizes do not: 1¼", 2", 3½".

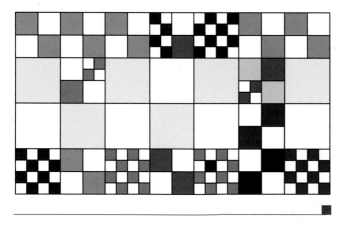

■ Make a checkerboard of two different colors, changing gradually into a combination of another two colors. Hand dyers frequently sell gradations that start with one color and metamorphose into another. Using two such gradations in four distinctly different colors makes constructing this kind of checkerboard much easier. See "Modulation" on page 76.

As is true of any brainstorming process, there is value in expounding idea after idea after idea, even if they are bad ideas. Bad ideas often generate better ones. Then, if you look at all of your terrible, bad, better, and good ideas, you'll find a few great ones. Artists who work in media other than quilting consider a success rate of forty percent fantastic. That means sixty percent is thrown in the trash! And in baseball, if a batter gets a hit three out of ten times he's at bat, he's a superstar!

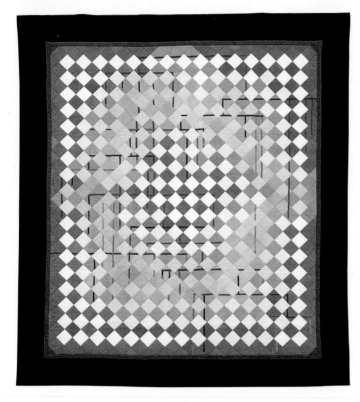

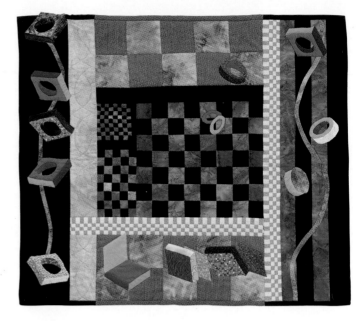

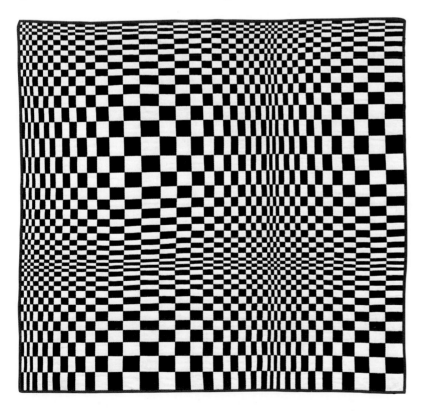

■ Untitled checkerboard by JoAnne Stroup, 1996, Camano Island, Washington, 29" x 25½". The small taupe- and-white checkerboard was pieced from a striped fabric and nicely echoes the larger checkerboards. JoAnne was influenced by shapes in a Katie Pasquini-Masopust book.

■ *A Light Balance* by Catherine Dawson, 1997, Calais, Maine, 55" x 63". Kate creates an intriguing illusion by superimposing the variegated checkerboard on top of the irregular grid of thin colored strips. The design is equaled by the technical tour de force of making it all match!

■ *Kinetic Curiosity* by Stephanie Cooper, 1988, Everett, Washington, 40" x 41". When strip widths change in incremental order, checkerboards can produce three-dimensional effects.

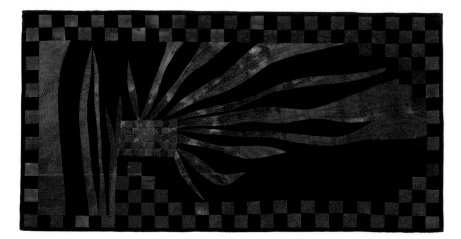

■*Modulation* by Lorraine Torrence, 1997, Seattle, Washington, 24½" x 32". This was an exercise I gave myself: turn a two-color checkerboard into a different two-color checkerboard. Two color gradations from DYEnamic Fabrics and Designs made it easy. One gradation changed from purple to teal, the other from fuchsia to yellow. I simply merged the two.

■*Italian Urns* by Reynola Pakusich, 1996, Bellingham, Washington, 39" x 49". A piece of Italian cotton was the beginning point for this varied-scale checkerboard quilt. Reynola unified the design by appliquéing a few squares over the print and using the print in the checkerboards.

■*Namaqualand Memory* by Louise Harris, 1997, Sedro Woolley, Washington, 32" x 16½". Judy Robertson's hand-dyed fabric is combined with a commercial black fabric in an unpredictable check. Notice that the checkerboards vary in scale.

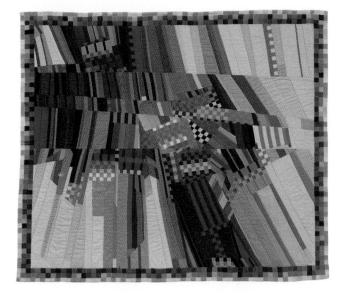

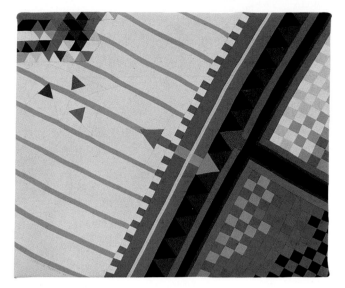

■ *Urban Camouflage* by Lorraine Torrence, 1991, Seattle, Washington, 60" x 52". I used sections of ¾" checkerboard and combined them with related elements (strips, stripes, and alternating squares) to provide variety. The border reintroduces the checkerboard theme through multicolored squares.

■ *Group Dynamics* by Lorraine Torrence, 1985, Seattle, Washington, 29" x 25". This is a pieced, but not quilted, silk noil quilt stretched on a frame. Many colors make up a rich checkerboard. (Collection of Laura Munson Reinstatler.)

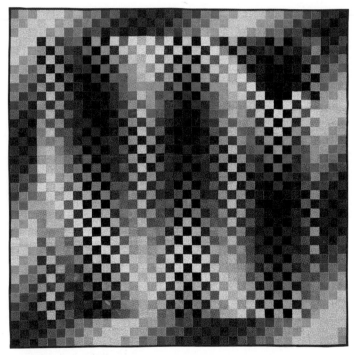

■ *Hale-Bopp* by Cathy Berk, 1997, Anacortes, Washington, 34" x 30". The pink diagonal comet checkerboard is a wonderful variation on the theme.

■ *Checkerboard* by Carol Roi Olsen, 1994, Bainbridge Island, Washington, 53" x 53". Carol made this checkerboard with her own hand-dyed fabrics after she took a class from Jan Myers-Newbury. The square size is constant throughout, but thanks to the color placement, the overall image is full of movement and life. The green in the border provides an "across-the-color-wheel" complement.

Help for Problem Quilts

If everything is running smoothly and you love the results of your labor, don't question it! Many quilters have an intuitive sense of color and design without having studied art. The time you actually need theory is when you are dissatisfied with your work. Then you can summon up your design vocabulary and figure out why your quilt isn't working and what you can do about it.

Nine times out of ten, there is a solution (or several) to a problem. The investment of precious time and fabric makes us reluctant to scrap what we've done and try something different. Unless you're doing Seminole patchwork, you probably shudder at the thought of taking your cutter to something you've already pieced, right? But if something about it bothers you, what are you gaining by leaving it the way it is? It will be nothing more than a painful reminder of many days spent toiling without reward. Just fix it!

What's Wrong?

First, ask yourself what you like and what you don't like about the quilt. Are the values so close you can't see the design? Does the color lack richness? Does the composition lack unity? Is there one really awkward shape in the midst of graceful ones? Is there no variety of scale?

Sometimes the answer is obvious. But at other times, you can't put your finger on it. When that happens, try lots of solutions. Do some visual brainstorming. Remember the "Fold-and-View" test for Multi-View Image quilts. (See page 59.)

Over the years as a quilting teacher, I've seen many quilters stare at an unsuccessful piece trying to decide what to do. Beethoven composed wonderful symphonies in his head without the benefit of hearing them, but most of us need to try out solutions and then evaluate them. *Make visual decisions visually!* Move things around, turn the piece upside down, hold colors up to substitute for those in the quilt.

I gathered a few quilts for this chapter that were in some way unsuccessful—pieces that fell short of evoking that "Yes!" response. In each case, a simple solution turned the piece around and made it better. See if you agree.

July 1, Hong Kong **by Lorraine Torrence**

At this stage of my "improved checkerboard" piece, I decided the background was too high in contrast, too busy to show the brightly colored sticks and streamers fused on top. I had even started satin stitching around the colored shapes before I admitted it wasn't working.

I considered several solutions for toning down the background: hand painting it, removing the fused shapes (they peeled right off), and overdyeing the background to make the white darker. I considered appliquéing charcoal gray over each white and partial square without

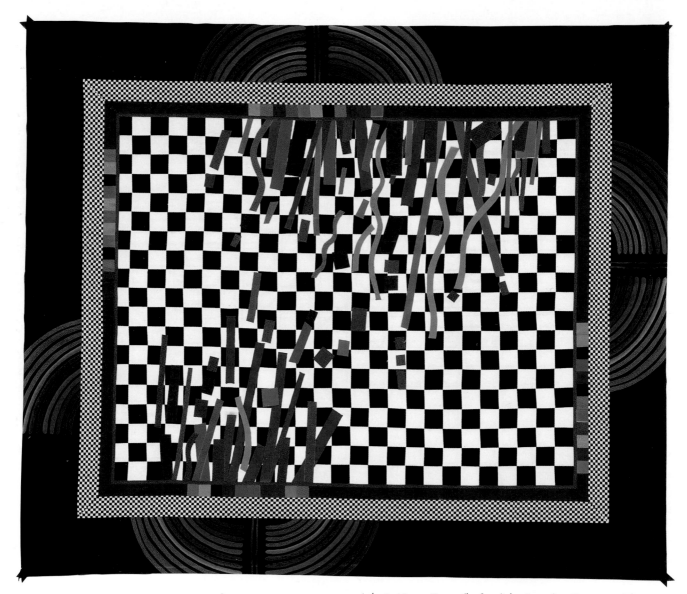

July 1, Hong Kong (before) by Lorraine Torrence. The background overpowers the colored streamers, and the border is rather ostentatious.

removing the colored shapes. I even thought about machine embroidering enough of the background to create an even-value background without completely obliterating the checkerboard.

I finally decided to remove the border, peel off the colored shapes that weren't already stitched down, and cover the checkerboard with two layers of white silk organza. I attached the organza with an irregular grid topstitched in cordonnet. Next, I re-fused the colored shapes on the organza and satin stitched them in place.

Of course, the placement of each piece was not exactly as it had been, but the general composition was the same, and the fusible web that remained on the colored shapes allowed me to reattach them easily.

This more subdued checkerboard provided a subordinate background for the dominant colored shapes. I simplified the border because the old one now seemed unnecessarily overdone.

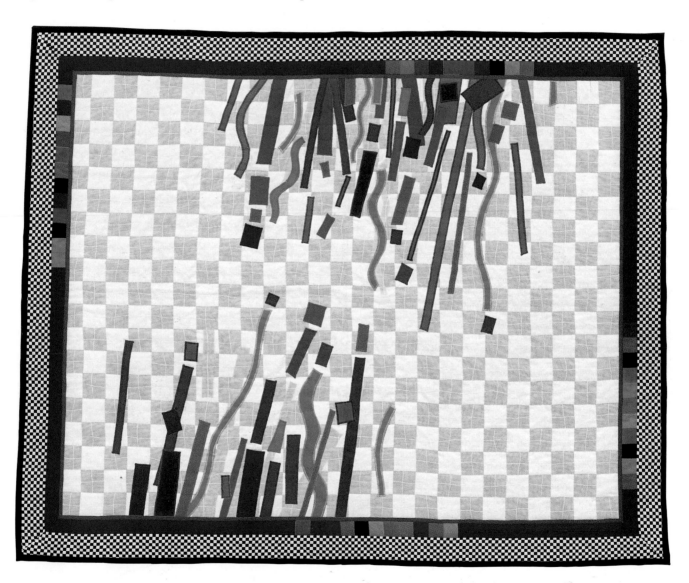

July 1, Hong Kong (after) by Lorraine Torrence, 1997, Seattle, Washington, 43¾" x 35½". Removing the border, peeling off the fused streamers, and covering the checkerboard with two layers of white organza toned down the background.

Facets Redux by Patrice Pelton

Patrice made this Multi-View Image quilt after her sister, who had taken my class, introduced the concept to her. She was dissatisfied with the quilt, but wasn't sure why. I suggested that the scale of the prints, as well as their values, were too similar to allow Patrice to read the terrific design.

Facets Redux (before) by Patrice Pelton. The values and scales of the printed fabrics are too similar for the beautiful design to be appreciated.

She had already layered and basted the quilt and started quilting, so we tried to think of improvements that wouldn't remove lots of stitching. Changing some of the fabrics would mean appliquéing the new fabrics on top of the old ones. She eliminated the option of turning under seam allowances and hand appliquéing. She also didn't want to turn under the edges and appliqué by topstitching with the same metallic thread used for the quilting.

Instead, Patrice chose to fuse new pieces to the quilt, leaving raw edges. Then she machine couched a decorative thread over the raw edges in a matching color. The lighter colors and less densely patterned fabric accentuated parts of the design, creating a different emphasis and balance. The higher-contrast design made the quilt more dramatic and both of us happier.

Facets Redux (after) by Patrice Pelton, 1997, Seattle, Washington, 38½" x 38½". Lightening some of the areas with less-patterned fabric made this design come alive. Patrice fused the additions to the quilt, then couched decorative thread over the raw edges. She didn't even have to use a seam ripper!

LISTENING ISLANDS BY DEANNA ARNESTAD

Here is a Single-Shape quilt that Deanna Arnestad designed in one of my classes. I liked the piece a lot as she developed it; Deanna had used wonderful colors and fabrics, nice variety of scale, and good movement. The quilt wasn't finished by the end of the class, and Deanna called me later saying she had come to an impasse and couldn't decide what to do next.

Listening Islands (before) by Deanna Arnestad. The red triangle is too centered and there is an awkward blunt line in the lower right. The upper left is too light in value to balance the rest of the quilt.

When we met, we agreed that adding another row of triangles along the top and left sides would offset the red triangle in the center of an otherwise asymmetrical composition. It would also give a little extra weight to the dark area in the upper left and balance the dark area in the lower right.

A blunt horizontal area at the lower right seemed to stop the beautiful diagonal movement in the rest of the quilt. Deanna changed the horizontal lines to diagonal ones and added a great border that incorporates movement from inside the quilt. A beginning design that had lots of merit became fabulous after just a few easy changes.

Listening Islands (after) by Deanna Arnestad, 1997, Everett, Washington, 35" x 47½". Deanna added a row of triangles across the top and along the left side of the quilt. This strengthened the top left area and moved the red triangle from the exact center. Deanna changed the blunt horizontal area to a diagonal line and added the border, which extended the design lines. Wonderful!

REVISED JUDGMENT BY SUE PELTON

The design of this Collage-Curves quilt was derived from the figure of a woman sitting at a desk, which Sue sketched because she found the shapes interesting. She abandoned the colors of the actual scene and substituted her favorite brights.

Sue's impulse was to accurately represent the shapes and lines of the subject matter, even though the quilt was stylized and abstract. The composition suffered for it. The

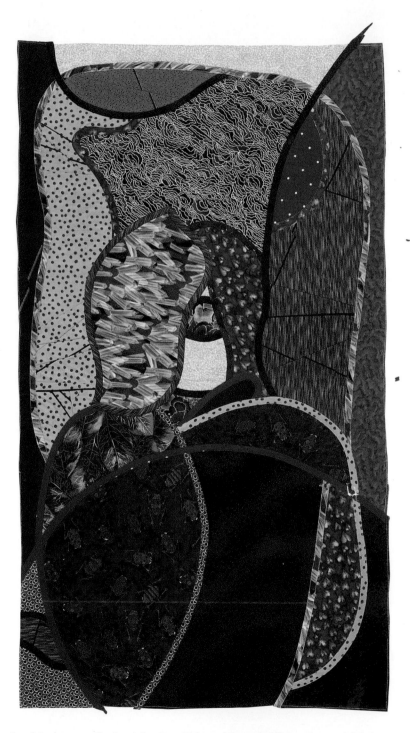

Revised Judgment (before) by Sue Pelton. Hmmm. Nice color and fabric, superb workmanship, but awkward composition.

bias-tape lines near and parallel to the edges pinched the space and stifled the movement occurring in other parts of the quilt. Sue folded the quilt in different ways to see how it would look with parts removed. She found an interesting area in the middle, a rectangle tipped at an angle, and cut it from the quilt. Sue was able to salvage the good elements and eliminate the less successful ones.

The corners of the new rectangle had to be filled in with parts that were trimmed from the other parts of the quilt. The result is a super little quilt with a variety of big, medium, and small spaces, plus dynamic diagonal movement and a nicely unified composition.

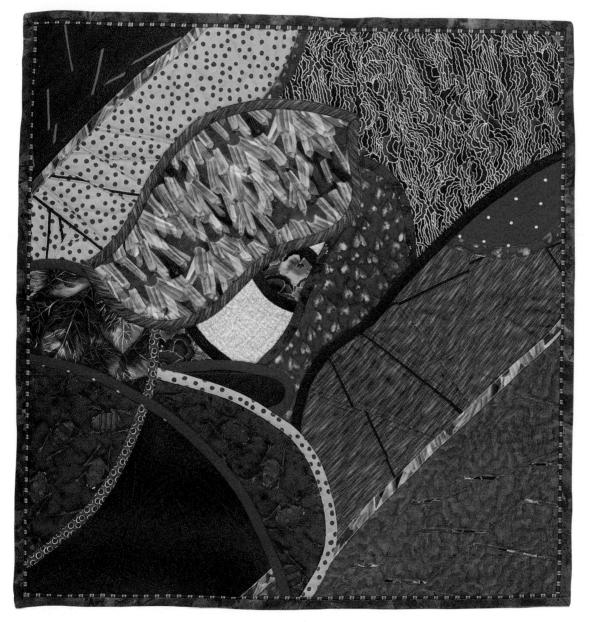

Revised Judgment (after) by Sue Pelton, 1997, Seattle, Washington, 26" x 24½". Cutting a rectangle out of the quilt and filling in the missing corners allowed a more dynamic composition to emerge. The varied sizes of the design elements started to perform their proper roles, and the diagonal movement created interest.

YUKATA CHECKERBOARD BY REYNOLA PAKUSICH

For an "Improving-the-Checkerboard" quilt, Reynola started with a beautiful Japanese yukata-cloth panel. She wanted to cut it into squares, remove every other square, and alternate the remaining squares with a checkerboard of new fabrics. She hoped it would create the illusion of looking through the new checkerboard to the yukata flower and leaves behind it. She was disappointed that the result was a low-contrast design in which there was no focal point.

To draw attention to the flower blossom, Reynola substituted dark purple squares for the brown squares that

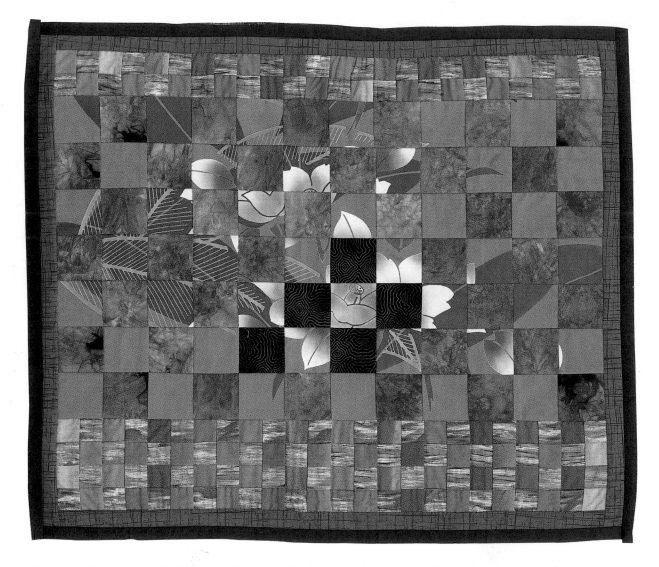

Yukata Checkerboard (before) by Reynola Pakusich. The flower in the yukata fabric disappears and the piece is muddy. Reynola felt her attempt to accent the flower with the dark squares was too heavy-handed. Now what?

originally surrounded the blossom. But she found this overpowered the delicate flower.

In an attempt to give validity to the dark purple, she repeated the hue in the first strips for what was to be a wider border. At that point, she stopped in dissatisfaction, feeling that these changes did not improve the quilt.

My suggestion was that she replace some of the alternating brown checkerboard squares with a lighter color—the creamy yellow. It might draw attention to the same hue in the veins of the leaves. I added a new arrangement of toned-down and varied squares to surround the flower blossom, and repeated the small scale of the little border squares in one or two places in the quilt's interior.

Reynola has superb artistic sensibilities and is a master of subtlety. She used my suggestions to kick-start a new solution and came up with an arrangement wonderfully different from mine. Here is her solution.

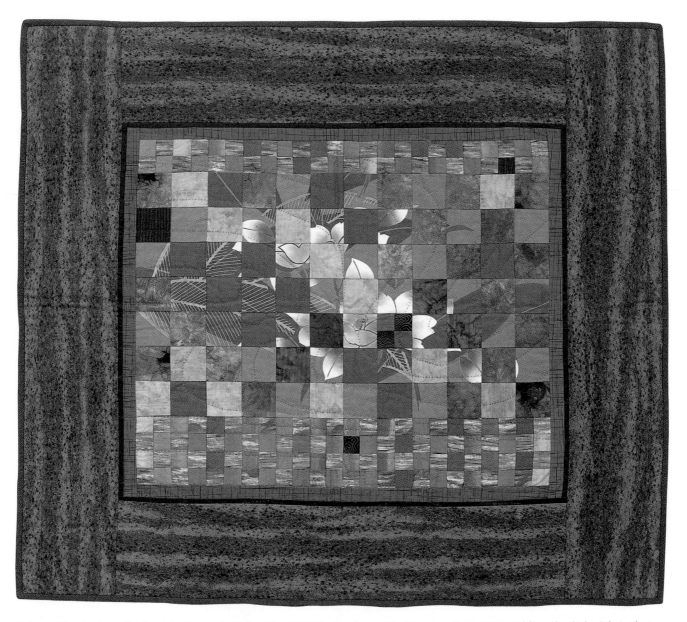

Yukata Checkerboard (after) by Reynola Pakusich, 1997, Bellingham, Washington, 34" x 30". Adding the light fabric that matched the leaf veins, softening the purple accents, and adding some small-scale squares to the large-squares area unified the design. Now we see light and graceful diagonal movement.

GROWING UP IN A DANGEROUS WORLD
BY LORRAINE TORRENCE

My Slash-and-Sew quilt is another example of poorly chosen background fabric. I thought the interesting spotty fabric was low-contrast enough to allow the floating shapes to dominate the composition. Even after I finished designing the quilt on my design wall, I felt the quilt was interesting in an unusual way. I plowed ahead and sewed it together. It was the most complex slash-and-sew quilt I had ever put together, and it kept me engaged and interested.

After I finished the top, I had nagging reservations, and finally decided the background was the problem. I knew I wanted to subdue the background without taking away all its interest. After all, there were some pretty big expanses of fabric with nothing but some intermittent seam lines interrupting them. I settled on a warm,

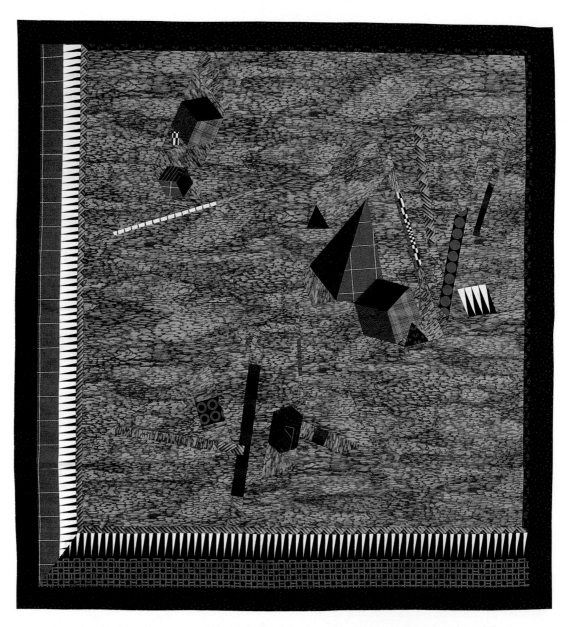

Growing Up in a Dangerous World (before) by Lorraine Torrence. It took me a while to decide I didn't like the background. The print is a little too busy.

concrete gray fabric paint that I mixed and applied directly to the background, but which left traces of the fabric showing. I was careful not to let my brush touch the floating shapes.

The paint only required heat setting with an iron, so it was simple for me, a designer who does not work with surface-design techniques. Reading Jane Dunnewold's book *Complex Cloth* (Fiber Studio Press, 1996), and consulting my quilting friend and fabric painter, Karen Perrine, gave me sufficient confidence to solve my problem.

The result is still more interesting than pretty, but I'm happy with how the design works as a whole. Subject matter and a title became clear to me—after the fact—as I looked at the background's jagged "concrete" roughness, combined with the toylike shapes and the piano-keyboard reference.

These are just a few examples of the solutions available to you to "fix" your less-than-perfect quilts. Usually there is something you can do with your failures beyond learning from your mistakes. Diana Swim Wessel, in her book, *Inspiration Odyssey* (Fiber Studio Press, 1996), writes of using pieced sections trimmed from one quilt as parts for another. If you can't make your quilt "work," why not cut it up and use pieces of it in a different quilt? On the rare occasion, however, that you are so unhappy with a piece that working on it is depressing, there is no reason to torture yourself. Do as I once heard Nancy Crow recommend: "Burn it!"

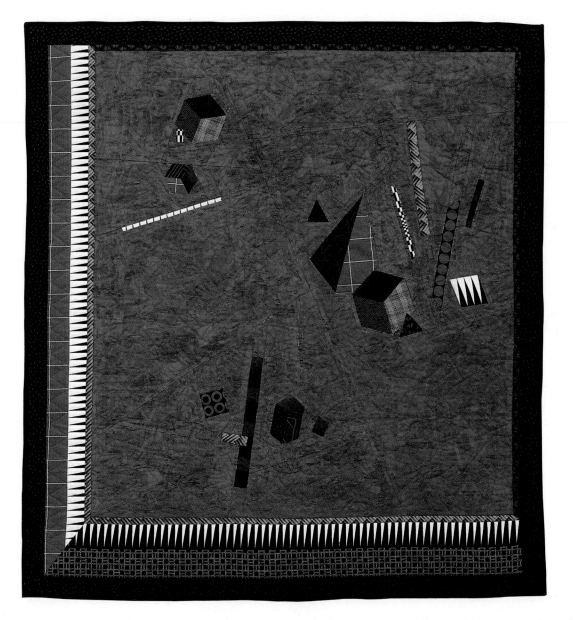

Growing Up in a Dangerous World (after) by Lorraine Torrence, 1997, Seattle, Washington, 44½" x 49". Painting the background fabric to make it slightly mottled but to read more as a solid made a big improvement. It looks like concrete, doesn't it?

Borders

Marguerite Ickis, in her 1949 classic *The Standard Book of Quiltmaking and Collecting*, wrote, "There is an old saying that the proof of the quilting ability lies in the border." In context, this is a reference to the technical ability to do a nice miter or design a motif that continues around a corner gracefully and identically to the other corners. But perhaps we can apply this old saying to how a border design relates to the body of the quilt.

Marguerite Ickis had this to say about borders:

A border, the dictionary tells us, is a boundary, or a margin or edge. It surrounds and hedges in, and also supports and protects what lies within the border. All these things are done for a quilt by its border. The border frames the pattern of the quilt as a picture is framed.

The rules which apply to picture framing are followed in selecting a border for the quilt. It must reflect and sustain the pattern, but not outshine it. A heavy ornate border on a dainty patterned quilt would be as unbalanced as a heavy carved gilt frame around a delicate pastel painting.

Marguerite's observations are as noteworthy today as they were then, nearly fifty years ago. Whatever you do in your border, enhance what is already there; do what the quilt needs, don't simply add dimension in a fast and easy way.

Consider the need for repetition (but with variety) to unify the design. Consider the need to vary scale. Consider the value in the border: Is it too dark to enhance an interior that is light to medium in value? Or is it too light for a dark interior?

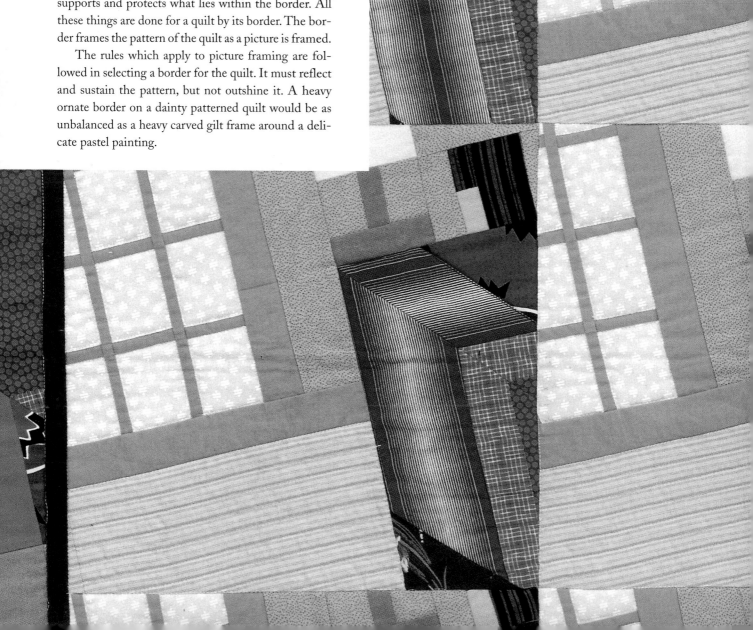

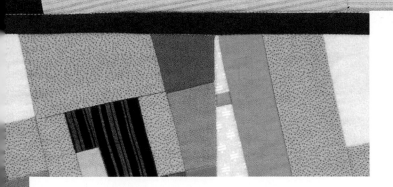

Another way to achieve the same look—no additional line of binding—is to sew the quilt top (with batting behind it) to the back of the quilt, right sides together, pillowcase fashion. I leave a 6"- to 8"-long opening, clip the corners, and turn the quilt right side out.

I often choose this finish when the quilt is small (45" x 60" or smaller) and has a simple border consisting of a narrow strip next to the body of the quilt, with a wider plain outer strip. If an additional narrow line in the form of a binding would be too much, I use this "pillowcase" edge so the quilt will end at its edge with no extra line.

No Borders

Occasionally I've looked at a quilt and felt that it didn't need another thing. The design was complete; nothing could make it any better. In such a case, I might want to face the edge. Facing is not my typical method, but it does finish the edge of a quilt without adding even a line of binding. I usually use a 1½"- to 2"- wide strip of fabric that is close in value and color to the quilt edge; sew it on the front of the quilt at the edge, one side at a time; understitch; then fold the facing to the back at the seam. I turn under the raw edge of the facing and hand stitch it to the back of the quilt.

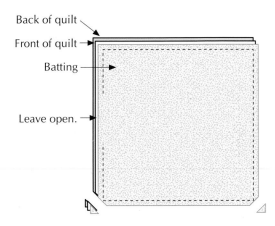

Back of quilt
Front of quilt
Batting

Leave open.

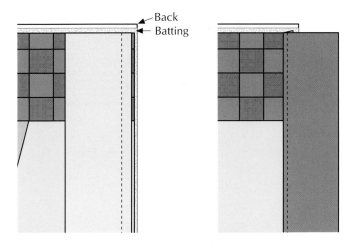

Back
Batting

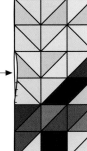

Hand stitch.

Back of quilt

Simple Borders

Miriam Kopec made a stunning Multi-View Image quilt in my class. (See "Untitled Multi-View Images" on page 65.) She kept all the trimmings left from cutting the blocks to produce the shifting image. But try as she might, she couldn't come up with a successful border using the trimmings. She had sewn a 2"-wide black border around the quilt and couldn't get any further. It was clear that her quilt was complete as it was.

Consider that your quilt may not need a border. If nothing you try helps the quilt, then audition a simple one- or two-strip border that will provide a simple frame. Place folded strips next to the quilt, refolding them a few times to try different widths. I am particularly fond of using a ¼"- or ½"-wide strip as a transition between the quilt and a plain wide border (or sometimes two narrow strips in different widths). Repeating one of the brighter, stronger colors of the quilt in the narrow strip can accomplish a color repetition or a variation in size, space, or scale, and can add pizzazz!

If you feel your quilt needs a complicated border to make it complete, here is a method I use for trying out different options. Take a snapshot of your quilt. The truer the color, the better, but you can "make do" with even a poor photo. Cut a hole in a plain piece of white paper the size and shape of the quilt in the photo. Tape the photo to the back of the white paper frame. (Use lift-off tape to remove the frame to try out other ideas.) Your "quilt" now has a white paper border.

Sketch a possible border on the white paper frame. Use colored pencils or markers to draw a border that enhances the interior of the quilt. Draw as many border ideas as you need to find the best option.

Look at the different border treatments throughout this book. Cover the border of a quilt with paper so you can see the quilt without the border. Look at the quilt again with the border exposed. Would you have added the same kind of border? How might you make it different? What are the design principles at work in the particularly successful borders?

As a final piece of advice on borders, try not to use up all your energy working on the interior of your quilt, then slap on a 6"-wide strip of solid black just to make the quilt bigger (unless, of course, that's exactly what the quilt needs!). Be willing to tackle a complicated border that will take lots of time if your quilt needs it. The quilt is not over till the border makes it sing!

Binding

The next, least noticeable, completion to the quilt's edge is a simple binding. If you feel that a ¼"- to ½"-wide line around the edge of your quilt is all it needs, then skip the border and just bind it. You may think a binding that blends smoothly in color and value is appropriate. Or perhaps a darker binding will contain and finalize best. In any case, try out possible choices by folding binding-fabric candidates around the edge of the quilt. Remember to make visual decisions visually! You'll know when you see it if you have chosen well or poorly. I always try to make binding out of a fabric that repeats an element in the interior of the quilt, or at least resembles one of the fabrics in the quilt.

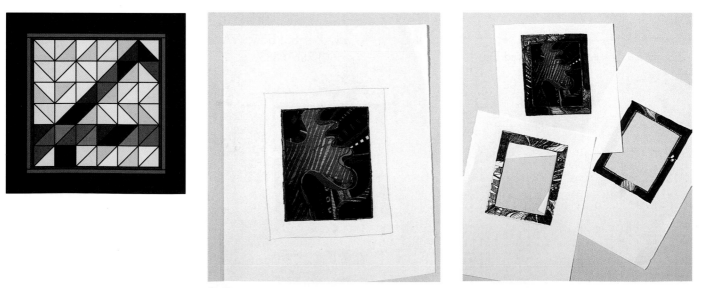

QUILT PHOTO WITH PAPER BORDER   **QUILT PHOTO WITH BORDER POSSIBILITIES**

Ethics

I'd like to address a subject that interests me greatly: ethics and courtesy in the quilt world. Never mind legality.

Through widespread sharing of information—by way of books, magazines, patterns, classes, and national conferences—we are provided with many opportunities to see quilts and absorb information. Internet bulletin boards and home pages on the World Wide Web make it possible to learn from quilters all over the world. Using other people's ideas was never easier. But this presents a smorgasbord of ethical questions we never had to worry about before.

Many quilters work with traditional patterns that are acknowledged to be in the public domain—patterns from anonymous forbears whose names will never be known. But other quilters are doing innovative work, developing techniques and designing one-of-a-kind art quilts. Some are professionals making a living in the quilt world as artists, designers, writers, teachers, lecturers, pattern makers, conference producers, consultants, editors, publishers, and shop owners.

In addition to me, most teachers I know use other teachers' techniques or ideas only after obtaining permission. Other teachers' handouts are off-limits without that permission. We are careful to give proper credit. Even casually acquired ideas are always credited to their originators, if possible. At the very least, when I don't know who originated a technique or idea, I try to let students know when an idea I present is not my own.

In the realm of exhibited work, standards are less clear. Like most quilters, I believe that work undertaken in a class under the direction of a teacher should not be entered in a competitive show. Nonjuried and nonjudged shows are appropriate venues for student work as long as proper acknowledgment of the source or inspiration appears along with the title and maker's name. Class work or work copied from books or patterns attributable to living, breathing human beings are inappropriate as entries in juried and judged shows.

Derivative work is not innovative work and should not be entered into competition as such. (In fact, there should be a line on quilt-show entry forms asking if the piece was derived from a class, book, pattern, or other source.) This way, the judges, who find it impossible to be informed about all activity in the quilt world and who may deliberate over two quilts, will know if one quilt is an original and one is a derivative work. Their decisions would reflect this information.

We can't help being influenced by each other. Do make it a priority to ask permission, give credit where it's due, and never, never pretend to be responsible for something someone else originated.

Resources

Many of the quilts shown in this book were made with hand-dyed fabric. If you don't dye fabric yourself and want to include it in your quilts, here are the dyers whose fabrics I have used with the greatest pleasure.

Hand-Dyed Fabrics

Arizona Colorwerks Hand-Dyed Fabric
Susanne Triplett
10835 North 45th Place, Phoenix, AZ 85028
e-mail:AZCW@aol.com
Wholesale inquiries only; available in many quilt shops.

Sonya Lee Barrington
837 47th Avenue, San Francisco, CA 94121
(415) 221-6510
Send $5.00 for swatches.

Cherrywood Fabrics, Inc.
Dawn Hall
PO Box 486, Brainerd, MN 56401
(218) 829-0967

DYEnamic Fabrics and Designs
PO Box 765, Columbia, SC 29202
Libit Woodington (803) 695-0307
Debby Griffis (803) 732-3388
Send $7.00 for a complete sample color card (includes $5.00 coupon good on future orders of $20.00 or more).

Just Imagination
Judy Robertson
PO Box 83, Bow, WA 98232
(360) 766-6885

Hand-Painted Fabrics

Skydyes
Mickey Lawler
83 Richmond Lane, West Hartford, CT 06117
Send #10 SASE for a sample swatch and order form or $26.00 for 12 sample pieces (9" x 11" each).

Machine-Washable, Hand-Dyed Silk

Pieces of Eight
Dianne Smith
PO Box 4306, South Colby, WA 98384
(360) 871-7756
e-mail: silk@silverlink.net

Bibliography

Allen, Ellen G. *Japanese Flower Arrangement.* Philadelphia: National Council Books, Inc., 1952.

Balosky, Andrea. *Transitions: Unlocking the Creative Quilter Within.* Bothell, Wash.: That Patchwork Place, 1996.

Barnes, Christine. *Color: The Quilter's Guide.* Bothell, Wash.: That Patchwork Place, 1997.

Bloomer, Carolyn. *Principles of Visual Perception.* New York: Design Press, 1990.

Clark, Kenneth. *An Introduction to Rembrandt.* New York: Icon Editions, Harper and Row, 1978.

Colvin, Joan. *The Nature of Design.* Bothell, Wash.: That Patchwork Place, 1996.

Dantzic, Cynthia Maris. *Design Dimensions: An Introduction to the Visual Surface.* Englewood Cliffs, N. J.: Prentice Hall, 1990.

Doheny, Marilyn. *Op-Art Quilts.* Edmonds, Wash.: Doheny Publications, 1996.

Dunnewold, Jane. *Complex Cloth.* Bothell, Wash.: That Patchwork Place, 1996.

Ickis, Marguerite. *The Standard Book of Quiltmaking and Collecting.* New York: Dover, 1959. Reprint of the 1949 Greystone Press publication.

Itten, Johannes. *Design and Form.* New York: Van Nostrand Reinhold, 1963 (rev. 1975).

———. *The Elements of Color.* New York: Van Nostrand Reinhold, 1970.

Kent, Sarah. *Composition.* New York: Dorling Kindersley, 1995.

Lauer, David. *Design Basics*, 3rd ed. Fort Worth: Harcourt Brace Jovanovich, 1990.

Malevich, Kasimir. *The Non-Objective World.* Chicago: Paul Theobold and Company, 1959. Translated from the original German published in 1929.

McDowell, Ruth. *Symmetry: A Design System for Quiltmakers.* Lafayette, Calif.: C&T Publishing, 1994.

Page, Hillary. *Color Right from the Start.* New York: Watson Guptill Publications, 1994.

Rand, Paul. *Design, Form and Chaos.* New Haven: Yale University Press, 1993.

Smith, Barbara Lee. *Celebrating the Stitch.* Newtown, Conn.: The Taunton Press, 1991.

Steele, Dr. William C., ed. *Flower Arrangement the Ikebana Way.* New York: Madison Square Press, Grossett and Dunlap, 1972.

Thiel, Philip. *Visual Awareness and Design.* Seattle: University of Washington Press, 1981.

Torrence, Lorraine. "With Your Permission." *American Quilter,* Spring 1994.

Wessel, Diana Swim. *Inspiration Odyssey.* Bothell, Wash.: That Patchwork Place, 1996.

Wolfrom, Joen. *The Visual Dance.* Lafayette, Calif.: C&T Publishing, 1995.

About the Author

Lorraine Torrence is a quiltmaker and wearable-art designer who lives in Seattle, Washington. She earned a B.F.A. from Ohio Wesleyan University and an M.F.A. from the University of Washington. Her garments have been in Fairfield Fashion Shows and American Quilter's Society Fashion Shows; in the latter, she has won several awards, including first place and the Award for Design Excellence. She has been teaching quiltmaking since 1972, when books on quiltmaking could be counted on one hand. This is her first book.